There is a great need for this book! Dr. Penfold has been uniquely prepared and gifted to write this book. He lays out a good foundation for the principles of reconciliation and walks the reader through the causes of conflict. Fortunately, he does not leave us there as he describes the practice of peacemaking. At this time, this book is needed more than ever before.

Edward E. Moody, Jr., Ph.D.
Executive Secretary of the National Association of
Freewill Baptists

Everything Dr. Penfold writes is helpful and practical. *Mending Fences: Reconciling Broken Relationships* is especially helpful because it is for everyday parishioners as well as church leaders. We all face conflict and need a biblical and practical path to resolution. I am keeping Chapter 11 ("Major Concepts for Reconciling Broken Relationships") on my desk for interventions in my ministry.

Brad Ransom
Chief Training Officer/Director of Church Planting
Free Will Baptist North American Ministries
Author of Creating Healthy Church Systems (RHP 2024)

I highly recommend this book! Conflict creates many problems in our world and impacts our families, churches, and businesses in many harmful ways. We all face conflict in our daily lives, but many of us are not sure how to resolve them.This book is a Biblically based, practical guide to work through conflict and to heal broken relationships from an experienced pastor and leader. As the Bible says - Blessed are the peacemakers - This book will guide you to bring peace to broken relationships.

Mike Chaney
Senior Vice President, Procter & Gamble (retired)

This book offers a wealth of helpful insights for Pastors and all Christians looking for Biblical solutions to conflicted relationships. I felt like I was sitting in a restaurant or living room having a lengthy conversation with Gordon about the challenges of resolving one of many types of conflict we find ourselves involved in, no matter if it's with a neighbor, church member, or business associate. I love that he injects his personal story of being reconciled with God and lays a clear theological foundation for the biblical principles he unpacks as he walks the reader through many different types of conflict. This book is not a theoretical, ivory tower reflection on this topic, but very real stories drawn from his wealth of experiences. Some conflicts are resolved, and some are not, which is both biblical and consistent with most people's experience. I think pastors and church leaders would benefit from this book as a helpful resource to turn to when they encounter conflict in their lives and want to see a biblical pathway forward.

David Wetzler
Founder of Church Smart Resources

This volume is a very powerful and effective blending of scriptural truths and wisdom Dr. Penfold gained from serving numerous congregations as a pastor, as well as counseling churches and pastors who are struggling. I highly recommend you read this book as you navigate personal relationships in this world.

Dale Leighty
CEO and Chairman of the Board
First National Bank of Colorado
Former Chairman of the Independent Community
Bankers of America

Mending Fences: Reconciling Broken Relationships answers a question we who lead in churches should be asking. How do we resolve conflict and regain the peace among ourselves that demonstrates we are God's people? Gordon, who has been on both sides of church conflict, has condensed years of experience into this book. Chapter 11 alone makes this a worthwhile addition to your reading list.

Dr. Steve Smith
President of Church Equippers Ministries

With the love of a father and the heart of a pastor, Gordon takes pen in hand to remind the reader of nothing less than the very heart of God itself: peace! To the professing believer lowering the gates of the heart and mind for the enemy of "needless strife" to sneak in, Gordon holds up the words of life and says, "Look! See!" To the employee whose resentment and anger grow daily and who never cultivates a peace-loving theology of work or joy, Gordon says, "Listen! Perceive!" Gordon reminds us that it is NOT the Father who sows discord among brothers and sisters—it is the enemy. Why join or help the enemy in his work? Why not instead use our time relentlessly pursuing the peace for which the Son gave His life? After all, those for whom Christ died are those with whom we will happily share eternity. Why not start practicing now? These are the piercing questions of Gordon's *Mending Fences*. Gordon's tone is not one of a reprimanding school Principal, but one of a pleading father. By God's grace, may the urgent message of this book reach far and wide, as we strive with all our hearts for the "Peace of God found only in the God of Peace."

Ian McFarland
Planter and Pastor
Cornerstone Community Church, Riverton, Wyoming

MENDING FENCES

MENDING FENCES

Reconciling Broken Relationships

Gordon E. Penfold

Mending Fences
Reconciling Broken Relationships

© 2025 Gordon Penfold.

ISBN: 979-8-9993592-1-6

Cover photo: Photo by Roger Starnes, Sr. on Unsplash.com

Formatting and Cover Kim Gardell, Gardell Design

DEDICATION

When we moved to Wyoming in June 1997, my daughter, Rachel, took a summer job near Cooke City, Montana. I visited her at the ranch. While there, a report came to the ranch foreman that the neighbor's cattle broke through a fence and roamed freely through their pasture, pasture reserved for grazing later that summer. Rachel and I joined the ranchers and enjoyed the privilege of riding through the ranch to gather the strays and herd them back to the neighbor's ranch. We discovered that the neighbors had already rounded up the cattle. However, we could tell where the cattle grazed. It was as if a lawnmower buzzed through the pasture. The cattle mowed all the verdant, green growth down to stubble.

The necessity of mending the broken fence became vividly apparent. In this case, good fences made for good neighbors. A broken fence, for MAD neighbors. What caused the break? Neglect? Age? Wild cattle? Intentional destruction? Many factors may have contributed to the break. But urgency demanded a response to repair the fence and the damaged pasture and hurt feelings.

In our lives, it is likewise true that mending fences is essential for maintaining great relationships regardless of the cause of the conflicts.

This volume is dedicated to peacemakers—those individuals who wade into the deep end of conflict without wavering. These courageous souls take on superhuman challenges in order to see relationships restored, peace reign, and to see broken fences mended. These unsung heroes do not find their names plastered in the headlines, nor do they receive great temporal rewards for the stewardship of their ministry, but they slog on through the muck and mire of conflict to see relationships transformed and harmony restored. The work is painful yet satisfying, gut-wrenching but joyful. The great reward is yet to come when their Savior and Master says to them, "Well done, good and faithful servant."

The need for peacemakers cries out from the crowds of broken people and broken relationships—in the home, in the church, among civic-minded groups and in businesses. May the Lord continue to raise people deeply touched by God's grace who can pass that grace along through their peacemaking efforts.

May you, the reader, become such an individual who strives to mend fences and repair broken relationships!

Saddle up. We've got work to do!

ACKNOWLEDGMENTS

As in any undertaking like this, many people contributed to the completion of this book. First, my wife Beth endured much as I focused time on this project. She also served at my side in numerous deeply conflicted churches. Her keen insights and sage counsel strengthened and protected me as no other could as we traversed the raging streams of conflict together!

When working with challenging conflict situations in churches, I always used teams. These team members also contributed much to the success of these ventures. I developed a team for each church, and I leaned heavily on their perceptions and understanding. Each one contributed to my growth, and that growth is visible in this volume.

I also wish to thank each church I served. Each unique family aided in my growth and development, albeit sometimes painfully so! First Baptist Church, Riverton and Faith Baptist Church in Parker both helped to hone and refine me, sharpening my skills in handling difficult situations. I'm grateful to both churches. As old wisdom states, "Disagreement is the abrasive that polishes the best ideas." God did a lot of polishing in me.

I am also grateful for Rev. Robert Humphry. Starting in 2003, Bob entrusted me with leading teams in deeply conflicted situations. He coached and mentored me through the whitewater and white knuckle times in a church's life. I'm profoundly thankful to him for setting me on this course as a peacemaker. Bob now resides in heaven, but the breadth and depth of his work continue.

Michael Hodgin gave himself to the work of editing. His passion for the work improved the book at every turn. I'm indebted to him and thankful for his genuine friendship and insights!

Finally, and most significantly, I thank our Lord Jesus Christ, the ultimate peacemaker. He made peace with me and now allows me to follow in His steps. Lord, I bless Your name with great thanksgiving and joy.

CONTENTS

PREFACE

It is with great delight that I write a volume like this. My varied background impacts my view of life and conflict. I worked blue-collar jobs throughout my high school and university years, and worked as a structural engineer for six and a half years. During this time, I became a registered professional engineer and maintained my registration for thirty years. However, the bulk of my experience comes from serving as a pastor. I served four churches as a full-time pastor and completed four intentional interim pastorates. I continue to work with pastors and churches through Fresh Start Ministries Network and Advanced Pastoral Network (APN) (formerly TAP, Inc.). Therefore, most of my writing will include examples from my ministry experience. However, I've seen the problems, principles and prescriptions described here at work in the marketplace, service clubs, higher education institutions, in our homes and local churches.

My first exposure to biblical conflict resolution occurred in 1977 when I became embroiled in a conflict issue as a young leader at a large church. We followed to completion the process outlined in Matthew 18:15-18. My interest in the subject was piqued when I began to teach in the Former Soviet Union (FSU) in 1994. I discovered that pastors and church leaders inappropriately used church discipline as a means of controlling their members. In the theology of evangelicals in the FSU, there is no salvation outside the local church. If one is excommunicated from a local congregation, they lose their salvation. To control the membership, church leaders threatened them with expulsion if church members did not knuckle under pressure exerted by the church leadership to control the congregation, leadership tactics that greatly resembled oppressive and repressive Soviet leadership. So, the people normally acquiesced to their less-than-sterling leadership. THIS IS NOT THE PROPER USE OF CHURCH DISCIPLINE! These abuses led me to a thirty-year study of the subject of conflict resolution and biblical peacemaking that included church discipline.

This prompted me to begin this quest to understand and properly apply the principles and practices of conflict resolution and biblical peacemaking.

My original title, "Mending Fences in the Home, the Church and the Marketplace," proved too broad for a single volume. Therefore, this book focuses primarily on issues that fit churches and Christ-followers.

Churches possess certain processes of accountability and recourse that are unavailable in the workplace or civic organization. A higher law binds believers in Jesus Christ—the Royal Law: "If you really fulfill the royal law according to the Scripture, 'You shall love your neighbor as yourself,' you do well" (James 2:8). This higher law, when applied, produces delightful outcomes, but when ignored, results in damaged relationships and less-than-stellar behavior.

Know that these powerful principles can impact and change lives and relationships. Throughout the book, I will mention churches, businesses, civic groups and interpersonal relationships. These outcomes described here may not occur as readily in the secular world as in churches. Nevertheless, practice the principles outlined in this volume, and you may be surprised by your attempts to mend fences and reconcile broken relationships.

Often, we are the ones who need God's touch. The reconciliation of broken relationships lies primarily within us, not others.

Conflict is ubiquitous. Most people chafe when faced with conflict. The typical responses to conflict are well known: fight, flight or freeze. Many turn a blind eye or a deaf ear to conflict challenges. The instructions in this book give people tools and principles that will enable them to navigate conflict and mend broken relationships. Our deeply divided world needs to apply these concepts of reconciliation.

Conflict produces great challenges and wonderful opportunities for growth. May you grow exponentially through the challenges you face!

Insight

For those who wish to get to the "good stuff" at the end of the book, please begin reading Chapter 7, Flash Points Contributing to Conflict. However, I feel that the foundations described at the beginning of the book for conflict resolution and biblical peacemaking are essential for your health and spiritual well-being.

My prayer for you, the reader, is that you will grasp the sweetness of joy of restoration between you and those with whom you rub shoulders in this journey called life. May the Peace of God and the God of Peace impact you deeply.

Gordon E. Penfold
June 8, 2024

INTRODUCTION

During one of my seventh-grade basketball games, I placed my hands just above my knees during a timeout. (That's what you do when you're tired and somewhat out of condition!) Suddenly, I felt ill. Just above my left knee, my thumb landed on a hard mass—a lump. I frantically squeezed my right leg, thinking there was no worry if I had a matching pair—only one. I don't remember what Coach Bachovitch said during the timeout. My mind raced as the significance of that mass on my leg over-whelmed my thoughts.

I didn't want to say anything to my parents. Our family had a history of cancer. A mixture of terror and frantic wondering gripped my heart! Three years earlier, I had my appendix re-moved the day after Thanksgiving. I spent a full week at Presbyterian Hospital in Denver (not at Children's Hospital) in a ward with about forty other patients, all much older than I. That experience left me with no taste for hospitals or doctors. I feared my parents would say, "We're taking you to the doctor," and he would say, "You're going to the hospital."

I finally built up enough courage to show my folks my leg. When they saw the bump, the color drained from their faces. Sure enough, they said, "We're taking you to the doctor." The doctor said, "I'm sending you to a bone specialist in Greeley."

While there, Dr. Arp said, "Gordon has the largest bone spur I have ever seen. It's about six inches long, growing out of his femur. (It looked like one scoop of a moose antler). We don't know what caused it. He may have been born with it, or it could be the result of an injury." Turning to my parents, he said quietly, "We won't know if it's malignant until we remove it." I knew what malignant meant. I also knew they could cut my leg off by inches if I had bone cancer, but eventually, I would die—one more childhood cancer victim. Bone cancer treatments were in their infancy in those days. I had no hope and no peace!

Several people came in to talk to me as I lay in a hospital bed awaiting surgery. Some wanted to make me laugh, and others wanted to engage in small talk. I remember not one of these individuals came to talk about spiritual things. The preacher from our church didn't show up. Looking back, he was not a Christ-follower, so he had nothing to offer me. If I were going to die, I wanted to know how to get to heaven. No one offered any hope. Most of my visitors felt awkward!

No cancer! Relieved. But a question still burned in the back of my mind. When I die, will I be in the smoking or non-smoking section, heaven or hell? I didn't know. That question haunted me all the way to college a few years later.

While at Colorado State University, I looked like an All-American guy. Doug Cannon, a man associated with the Navigators, a Christian discipleship organization, feared to approach me because he thought, "What can I offer this guy? He's tall, blonde, and good-looking (his assessment, not mine. He hit two of the three—tall and blond). He's got his life all together."

I didn't have it all together. People viewed me outwardly when I smiled or laughed, not knowing that I was hiding my insecurities.

I studied like every other engineering student. But inwardly, I wondered, "What will come when my life ends? I realized there had to be more to life than just earning a paycheck. As a cartoon caption said, "I have an alarm clock that tells me when to get up. I need one to tell me why!" I needed to know why I existed.

I appeared like the Pharisees in the first century who looked "good!" Jesus said, "You are like whitewashed tombs—beautiful on the outside, but full of dead men's bones and all uncleanness" (Matthew 23:27). That was an apt description of me. I looked great on the outside but was dead on the inside. Underneath my façade, I had no peace about my future.

Then on March 23, 1969, Dick Kreider and Wally Johnson, some other men associated with the Navigators, clearly shared the gospel with me—"that Christ died for my sin according to the Scripture, He was buried and rose again the third day according to the Scripture, and he was seen alive...." (1 Corinthians 15:1-8). I was not convinced when I heard the gospel. It was a foreign concept to me, even though I attended church regularly for my first eighteen years of living! I was so bold that I told them I thought they were crazy.

During the next week, I could not get the name of Jesus Christ out of my mind. It was as though His name was burned into my consciousness. On Friday morning, as I stood before the mirror in our dorm room, I saw myself clearly for the first time. I said to myself, "Penfold, your problem is you're a sinner." My mind raced as I thought of the implications of my declaration.

On my way to class, I managed to pick a pair of shoes out of my closet that didn't match. I also managed to pick a mismatched pair of socks. As I walked head down, I noticed my wardrobe malfunction on my way to the Engineering building. I hoped that no one else would see my feet. I looked to see if anyone else observed my faux pas. As I surveyed the hundreds of faces across the Plaza that morning, not one person held their head up. They all intently looked at the ground in front of them. I'm sure many found themselves deep in thought, facing the same predicament that I faced. They were living but lacked purpose and meaning in life. The sad affect etched on their faces demonstrated the deep emptiness I sensed.

However, on March 28, 1969, I placed my faith in Jesus Christ as my Savior and Sin-bearer. My quest for peace ended. I knew that the smoking section of eternity was off-limits to me.

Billy Graham, in his book *Peace With God,* says this. "These three facts constitute the true story of man; his past is filled with sin; his present is overflowing with sorrow; and the certainty of death faces him in the future."[1] When I trusted Christ, all three issues were settled. Christ paid the debt of my sin, joy replaced sorrow, and my future in heaven became clear. My disconnect with God ended. I also discovered genuine people when I entered this relationship with Christ.

Today, I see the same absence of genuine peace all around me. Everywhere we turn, people are upset. There are upsets with politics (worse than I ever remember, and I remember a lot), upsets in the home, upsets in the church and upsets in the marketplace. Everyone and every place seems to be suffering through upheaval, and that is not advantageous for any of us.

All of these upheavals became accentuated in March 2020 because of COVID-19.[2] The "Rona" has turned all that we knew

---

1   Billy Graham, *Peace With God* (New York, Pocket Books, 47th Edition, 1974), 11-12.

2   The content of the following section was suggested by Ed Stetzer in a podcast with Vibrant Congregations, https://vibrantcongregations.org/church-now-conversations-season-2/ed-stetzer-2/, April 17, 2022. The development of the material is my own.

inside out. The resulting changes make everyone edgy. We all want to get back to normal—whatever normal is—but that's not happening! Change is hard, unsettling and frustrating. Our emotions often erupt from pent-up anxiety, the anxiety produced by external change.

Here are some present realities we face.

Distrust and Mistrust. Many individuals can no longer speak to others with civility. Hot tempers and inviolable positions shred families. This mistrust engulfs families torn over political division, police departments over arrests and deaths of prisoners in custody, and neighbors over political preferences, gun rights, gay rights, and parental rights. Even siblings become alienated from one another. Parents and children face a growing crisis so that even times of family gatherings at Thanksgiving and Christmas become dreaded moments of anxiety as we wait for the "fights" to begin. Or for the next shoe to fall. Rather than making beautiful memories that will last a lifetime, we leave exhausted after walking on eggshells. People no longer converse with one another. One of two reactions occurs. When they do speak, they shout at one another or don't speak at all! It happens in my family. I'll bet it happens in your family, too!

Fractured Families. In a recent conversation, a friend mentioned "children divorcing their parents." This came as a shock to me. I know many families where deep struggles occur between children and their parents. I see the pain that grandparents face when their children refuse to let them visit and interact with their grandchildren. This tragic, painful reality tears up parents who long for a normal relationship with their children and grandchildren.

How prevalent is estrangement? Some studies suggest that over 25 percent of the U.S. population is estranged from a relative. This figure shows that in America, we have a huge problem with seriously broken relationships. What are some of the causes of estrangement?

- A child's spouse has serious disagreements with their in-laws.
- Physical, emotional or sexual abuse
- Domineering parents
- Poor choices on the part of children or parents
- Favoritism

This list is not exhaustive by any means. My heart aches for families who find themselves in the depths of brokenness.

In the case of divorce between a child and parents, formal and legal action takes place that makes "estrangement" enforceable by law. In these cases, the child formally "divorces" his parents and prohibits interaction between parents, children and grandchildren.

In our conversation, my friend stated that a legal "divorce" took place between the parents and their son and his wife. The son and family moved several states away from their parents. After two years, the grief-stricken mother/grandmother traveled to see the family and to seek reconciliation. She found their house and waited a couple of hours to make certain this was her family. Finally, she walked to the front door, knocked and waited. Her daughter-in-law answered the door and promptly called the police, who arrested the woman. The courts issued a restraining order against the mother and warned her that jail time awaited her if she attempted to contact her family again.

I cannot imagine how people exist in the pain of these deeply broken situations. Are you one of these people living in deep agony over broken relationships? Do you long to mend fences?

Social Media. All the focus on social media pushes people to their limits. Social media compels us to post the perfect glam shot, perfect face and perfect life. Last time I checked, no one filled the "perfection" bill. Look in the mirror! The pressures brought to bear on young people overwhelm them. Billy McMahan, a friend who works with teens, notes that even in junior high, teenagers feel the pressure to be perfect. They panic in junior high if they receive a "B" on their report card because that "B" may sink their chances of attending the school of their dreams. Whatever happened to just being a teen?

The Gender Debate. And then we have the whole gender debate. Again, tremendous pressure falls on children as young as primary school. Confusion abounds in what should be a simple understanding of how God made us in His likeness and image— male and female. Kyle Meeker cogently argues that even a person's soul and body are united in their identity.[3]

Mental Health. Mental health challenges abound, in part because of the difficulties mentioned above. In the summer of 2022, I learned of the suicide of a dear friend and his wife from my hometown. Their passing left a gaping hole in the hearts of all who knew them. Another classmate mentioned, "I might choose the same option for myself?" I pleaded with him, "Please do not consider this. Suicide doesn't just affect you. The carnage of suicide leaves deep wounds and lifelong scars with family and friends."

---

3   Kyle M. Meeker, "Souls Are Gendered: The Underappreciated Gift of our Integrated and Integral Gender-Identity." Evangelical Theological Society, San Antonio, Texas, November 14, 2023. At the creation, God made people male and female (Genesis 1:27). Meeker cogently argues that even our souls are gendered. A male soul corresponds to a male body, and a female soul corresponds to a female body. Neither time nor eternity change our gender identity.

Ethnic Tensions. Then, there is the issue of "race" relationships. I'm thankful the Bible is clear that there is only one race—the human race. We come in all shapes and sizes, but we still bleed red. Nevertheless, injustice creates much apprehension. One of my pastor friends says, "We're all prejudiced." He's probably correct. In the 1990s, Promise Keepers bridged the gap between people groups. I'll never forget singing together at Mile High Stadium in Denver as 86,000 raised their voices to praise our Lord Jesus Christ. We looked like salt, pepper and chili peppers scattered through the stands! I long for that day to return. I can get back to that old "normal!"

Social Unrest. I'm somewhat accustomed to unrest and anger, though I've never enjoyed it. These days remind me of my teen and early adult years in the 60s. Those trying days, filled with protests and violence, made a deep impression on my generation. For example, Beth (my future wife), her roommate Eva, and I sat at Moby Arena on the campus of Colorado State University during a basketball game between Brigham Young University and Colorado State University. Tensions ran high because, in those days, BYU and the Mormons refused to admit that black people had souls. A melee erupted in the gym. During the scrum, someone threw a six-inch piece of angle iron out of the stands and hit a policeman in the back of his head. His helmet saved his life, though he sustained a significant injury. Another angry individual threw a Molotov cocktail onto the gym floor. Fortunately, the bottle did not break and cause a fire in the packed arena. The three of us hastily left the event, our souls marred by the terrible unrest. Later, in the spring of 1970, someone torched "Old Main," one of the original buildings on campus. Violence marked the sleepy berg known as Fort Collins. Innocence lost. Grief overwhelmed.

Like today, murders, assassinations and racial unrest tore deeply at the fabric of our souls. Nevertheless, amid all the chaos, the Jesus Movement took root in California. Promise Keepers began in the 1990s. For a season, mending fences and restoring broken relationships started to permeate many levels of society.

No matter when we live or how much issues in life change, they tend to remain the same. Listen to the words of Habakkuk, the Prophet, who lived and wrote in the 7th Century BC.

> O LORD, how long shall I cry, and You will not hear? Even cry out to You, "Violence!" And You will not save. Why do You show me iniquity and cause *me* to see trouble? For plundering and violence *are* before me; **There is strife, and contention arises. Therefore, the law is powerless, and justice never goes forth**. For the wicked surround the righteous; Therefore, perverse judgment proceeds.
> —Habakkuk 1:2-4 (author's emphasis)

His lament reminds me of my own. In times like his and ours, we need to learn how to navigate the treacherous terrain of conflict and unrighteousness with grace and hope. Otherwise, we risk being swallowed up by the unsettling forces of the day.

I long for a time when we can become civil with one another, a time when we can mend broken fences at home, in the marketplace, and even in the church. I'm thankful you chose to join me on this journey. This trek for peace begins with The God of Peace and The Peace of God!

PART 1

Foundational Principles for Mending Fences

- ▶ PEACE DEFINED
- ▶ THE GOD OF PEACE
- ▶ THE PEACE OF GOD
- ▶ CONFLICT EXPLORED

CHAPTER 1

PEACE DEFINED

The word "peace" occurs in 368 verses and is used 399 times in the New King James Version of the Bible. You will discover similar totals in any reliable translation of the Scriptures. *Shalom* (the Hebrew word for peace) and other derivatives of this root occur 303 times in the Old Testament, and *irēnē* (the Greek word for peace) and its derivatives are used in 88 passages, with 96 uses of this root in the New Testament. The word "peace" occurs in every New Testament book except 1 John and in every Old Testament book except Ruth, Nehemiah, Hosea, Joel, Jonah, Habakkuk, and Zephaniah. The most frequent usage is in Leviticus, where Moses uses the word thirty-two times primarily to describe peace offerings in Israel's worship.

Elwell summarizes peace in this manner.

Total well-being, prosperity, and security associated with God's presence among his people. Linked in the OT [Old Testament] with the covenant, the presence of peace, as God's gift, was conditional upon Israel's obedience. In prophetic material, true peace is part of the end-time hope of God's salvation. In the NT [New Testament], this longed-for peace is understood as having come in Christ and able to be experienced by faith.[4]

Foulkes in the New Bible Dictionary explains *shalom*.

Basically, the OT word for peace, šālôm, means 'completeness,' 'soundness,' 'well-being.' It is used when one asks of or prays for the welfare of another (Gn. 43:27; Ex. 4:18; Jdg. 19:20) when one is in harmony or concord with another (Jos. 9:15; 1 Ki. 5:12) when one seeks the good of a city or country (Ps. 122:6; Je. 29:7). It may mean material prosperity (Ps. 73:3) or physical safety (Ps. 4:8). But also, it may mean spiritual well-being. Such peace is the associate of righteousness and truth, but not of wickedness (Ps. 85:10; Is. 48:18, 22; 57:19-21).

In classical Greek, *eirēnē* had a primarily negative force, but by way of the lxx [Septuagint], the word in the NT has the full content of the OT šālôm and nearly always carries a spiritual connotation. The breadth of its meaning is especially apparent from its linking with such keywords as grace (Rom. 1:7, *etc.*), life (Rom. 8:6), righteousness (Rom. 14:17), and from its use in benedictions such as 1 Thes. 5:23 and Heb. 13:20f. (*cf.* 2 Pet. 3:14).

For sinful man, there must first be peace with God, the removal of sin's enmity through the sacrifice of Christ (Rom. 5:1; Col. 1:20). Then inward peace can follow (Phil. 4:7), unhindered by the world's strife (Jn. 14:27; 16:33). Peace between man and man is part of the purpose for which Christ died (Eph. 2) and of the Spirit's work (Gal. 5:22); but man must

---

4   Elwell, W. A., & Beitzel, B. J. (1988). "Peace." In *Baker Encyclopedia of the Bible* (Vol. 2, p. 1634). Grand Rapids, MI: Baker Book House.

also be active to promote it (Eph. 4:3; Heb. 12:14), not merely as the elimination of discord, but as the harmony and true functioning of the body of Christ (Rom. 14:19; 1 Cor. 14:33).[5]

Interestingly, the prophets Isaiah and Jeremiah use peace more frequently than any other Old Testament books (33 and 25 times, respectively) amid the chaos of the threatened Babylonian invasion. These books emphasize the forfeiture of peace because of Israel's continued disobedience to the Lord! For example, Jeremiah 8:15 states, "*We* looked for **peace**, but no good *came;* and for a time of health, and there was trouble!" Peace is precious to those who experience it but remains absent from the lives of those who reject God's purposes for themselves.

A friend, Van Minter, pastor of Lakeridge Bible Church, Mesquite, Texas, gave this definition of peace. "Peace is a state of wholeness and completeness that impacts our relationship with God, others, and ourselves."[6] I like this definition because it deals with interpersonal relationships, our relationship with God, and us. Great relationships are a huge part of a life with peace!

Our Lord Jesus Christ declared these promises to his disciples in John 14:27.

> Peace I leave with you, My peace I give to you; not as the world gives do I give to you. Let not your heart be troubled, neither let it be afraid.

---

5   Foulkes, F. (1996). Peace. In D. R. W. Wood, I. H. Marshall, A. R. Millard, J. I. Packer, & D. J. Wiseman (Eds.), *New Bible Dictionary* (3rd ed., p. 891). Leicester, England; Downers Grove, IL: InterVarsity Press.

6   Van Minter, in a sermon at Lakeridge Bible Church, Mesquite, Texas, June 27, 2021.

This passage presents several wonderful truths. First, the Lord grants peace to His followers! Second, the world cannot offer genuine peace; only Christ can produce this! We certainly see the lack of peace in the empty expressions of many around us.

Third, the Lord asks us to apply the following truth to our lives. "Don't be overwhelmed with all that comes your way, and don't be afraid!" Great promises for those of us who tend to surrender to the temptation to fret and void the peace God offers us!

As we launch into the satisfying journey of making peace through mending fences, we must first understand that peace originates with a genuine relationship with the God of Peace. Second, we can experience the Peace of God, a deep sense of peace rooted in His very being. First, let's look together at these six statements where God is called "the God of Peace."

CHAPTER 2

THE GOD OF PEACE

Six times in Scripture, God is designated as the "God of Peace." Each adds a special element to our understanding of our Great Creator God and His relationship to peace! Each section below begins with a quotation of a passage related to "the God of Peace," followed by an explanation.

- **The God of Peace is Present With Us**
- **The God of Peace Will Destroy the Enemy of Peace**
- **The God of Peace Journeys with Those Who Pursue Godliness**
- **The God of Peace Transforms and Preserves Us**
- **The God of Peace Completes Us in Christ**
- **The God of Peace Imparts Peace to Us**

The God of Peace Is Present With Us

Now, **the God of peace** be with you all. Amen.
—Romans 15:33

The Apostle Paul reminded his fellow Christ-followers in Rome of the presence of the God of Peace, the One who produces peace in us. The Roman Empire did not like Christianity for it claimed only One God and His Name was not Caesar! As we traverse through life, the Lord is with us. As Jesus promised, we have tribulation in the world, but amid the clamor and upsets of our world, we can enjoy peace. Hebrews 13:5 tells us that the Lord "will never leave you nor forsake you." Amid all opposition to the gospel and all the garbage the world throws at us, believers can rest in the God of Peace! We ought not to allow others to dictate the conditions for our peace. Only the Lord can provide that peace! Romans 15:33 concludes with "Amen"—Let it be so!

The God of Peace Will Destroy the Enemy of Peace.

And **the God of peace** will crush Satan under your feet shortly. The grace of our Lord Jesus Christ be with you. Amen. —Romans 16:20

Ironically, the God of Peace will destroy the enemy of peace, for the only way to experience ultimate peace requires the destruction of Satan himself. In the meantime, we get to "enjoy" the fruit of chaos while awaiting the fulfillment of this promise. Satan knows his time is limited, and he intensely stirs up strife, perhaps even more so today, knowing that the time of his freedom is growing short.[7]

The God of Peace Journeys with Those Who Pursue Godliness

Finally, brethren, whatever things are true, whatever things *are* noble, whatever things *are* just, whatever things

---

7   Satan knows his reign of terror will come to an end. Revelation 20:1-2 describes his coming imprisonment for 1,000 years. Then, after a brief fling of freedom, he will be cast in the Lake of Fire (Hell) forever..

are pure, whatever things *are* lovely, whatever things *are* of good report, if *there is* any virtue and if *there is* anything praiseworthy — meditate on these things. The things which you learned and received and heard and saw in me, these do, and **the God of peace** will be with you.
—Philippians 4:8-9

From prison in Rome, the Apostle exhorts the followers of the Lord Jesus Christ to follow the example he set. This example includes thinking noble thoughts and actions, pure, lovely and of good report. He concludes by saying, "If there is any virtue, and if there is anything praiseworthy—meditate on these things" (Philippians 4:8). The God of peace desires that we embrace these attitudes. As the adage states, "God loves you just the way you are, but He's not content to leave you there!" The fruit of this pursuit allows us to walk in the privileged company of the God of peace!

The God of Peace Transforms Us and Preserves Us

Now, may **the God of peace** Himself sanctify you completely, and may your whole spirit, soul, and body be preserved blameless at the coming of our Lord Jesus Christ.
—1 Thessalonians 5:23

In this passage, A. T. Robertson states this about the God of Peace. "The God [is] characterized by peace in his nature, who gladly bestows it also."[8]

---

8   Robertson, A. T. (1933). *Word Pictures in the New Testament* (1 Th 5:23). Broadman Press. https://ref.ly/logosres/LLS:46.50.2?off=2634264.

Today, great confusion exists among believers in understanding the concepts of justification and sanctification. Justification occurs at the moment we place our trust in Christ as Savior and Sin-bearer. The Lord declares us righteous, forgiven and seated already in heavenly places (Ephesians 2:4-6)! On the other hand, sanctification, the lifelong process of becoming more like our Savior, occurs continually as we walk with Him. The great news: The Lord constantly works to conform us to His likeness. He faithfully files and smooths our rough edges as He ultimately prepares us to enter His visible presence. Ironically, pain often accompanies us on this journey. The God of Peace shapes us and preserves us in the journey.

The God of Peace Completes Us in Christ

Now may **the God of peace** who brought up our Lord Jesus from the dead, that great Shepherd of the sheep, through the blood of the everlasting covenant, make you complete in every good work to do His will, working in you what is well pleasing in His sight, through Jesus Christ, to whom be glory forever and ever. Amen. —Hebrews 13:20-21

This passage adds to the previous text regarding sanctification. The phrase "make you complete" uses the Greek term *katartizo*. Bauer, Arndt, Gingrich, and Danker define *katartizo* this way. "1. Put in order, restore. Complete, make complete. Fully trained. 2. Prepare, make, create, design. The word is used to speak of fishermen repairing their nets (Matthew 4:21), or of restoring a fallen brother (Galatians 6:1), or of setting a broken bone."[9] Thus, the Lord constantly works to equip and adjust our Christian character to make us fully adequate to accomplish our Divine Design![10]

The God of Peace Imparts Peace to Us

So Gideon built an altar there to the Lord and called it **The-LORD-Is-Peace** (in Hebrew, *YWVH Shalom*—Jehovah is peace). (Judges 6:23)

This remarkable account (Judges 6:11-40) reveals Gideon's encounter with the God of Peace (in theological terms, this is a theophany—a physical appearance of God to a person). First, the Angel of the Lord calls Gideon a "Mighty Man of Valor." Gideon viewed himself as anything but a mighty man! He possessed a low view of himself and his family. He considered himself the least esteemed in his family and his family, the weakest clan in the Israeli tribe of Manasseh. Nevertheless, the Lord appointed him as a Judge over Israel to deliver the wayward nation from a vast horde comprised of Midianites and people from the East who were, at that moment, invading Israel. Because of Gideon's encounter with the Angel of the Lord, Gideon felt certain that he would die (Judges 6:22-23), for Israelites felt that certain death awaited anyone who saw God! Yet the God of Peace empowered this cowardly man and transformed him into a powerful leader and deliverer. Such can be the effect of the God of Peace on the timid heart. Through God's peace, the weak become mighty!

---

9   Walter Bauer, F. Wilbur Gingrich, William F. Arndt, and Frederick W. Danker, *A Greek-English Lexicon of the New Testament and Other Early Christian Literature*, 2nd ed. [Chicago: University of Chicago Press], s.v. katartizo).

10   For a discussion on Divine Design, see Aubrey Malphus and Gordon E. Penfold, *Re:Vision—The Key to Transforming Your Church* (Grand Rapids, Baker, 2014), 55-62.

Points to Ponder

1. What trials or traumas are you currently experiencing? Write them down.

2. Where do you struggle the most?

3. You cannot overcome your challenges alone. You need the power of the God of Peace to set you free! How can you respond to the God of Peace right now?

CHAPTER 3

THE PEACE OF GOD

Not only is God the God of Peace, but He desires that we experience the Peace of God—even amid the chaotic world in which we live. The peace He provides can filter into every nook and cranny of our being. God's Designs for Peace include four elements.[11] We will see that God desires us to 1) have peace with Him, 2) have inner peace, 3) have peace with one another, and 4) live at peace even with our enemies, those we call "difficult people." Sometimes, we discover that those problematic people are us!

- **Peace with God Through Christ**
- **Inner Peace**
- **Peace with One Another**
- **Peace with Our Enemies**

Peace with God Through Christ

The first step toward living a life of peace begins with a relationship with God found only in Jesus Christ. The following passage provides us with the foundation of this peace:

---

11   Ken Sande, *The Peacemaker: A Biblical Guide to Resolving Personal Conflict* (Grand Rapids, Baker, Third Ed, 2004), 43-47. Sande identifies three dimensions of peace. He includes the first three that I cover. I add a fourth: God desires us to be at peace with our enemies

For it pleased *the Father that* in Him [Christ], all the fullness should dwell, and by Him to reconcile all things to Himself, whether things on earth or things in heaven, having made peace through the blood of His cross.
–Colossians 1:19-20

Let's unpack this passage a bit. First, we see both God the Father and God the Son involved in this peacemaking process. Foundational to this concept is God's basic problem with humanity—sin. In Genesis 3, Adam rebelled against God's authority when he chose to eat the forbidden fruit. That single act of disobedience impacted all of Adam's descendants, all of humanity, as is seen in Romans 5:12. "Therefore, just as through one man sin entered the world, and death through sin, and thus death spread to all men because all sinned." The language of this text tells us that all of Adam's actions impacted all of Adam's descendants. We were with him and in him! Consequently, every person finds himself separated from God just as Adam found himself separated and hiding from God (Genesis 3:8).

Second, Christ's ministry reconciles people to God (Colossians 1:20). To be reconciled (Greek— ἀποκαταλλάξαι)[12] conveys the idea that a person's relationship with God changes completely. Baker's Encyclopedia of the Bible explains reconciliation clearly.

Restoration of friendly relationships and of peace where before there had been hostility and alienation. Ordinarily,

---

12   Robertson, A. T. (1933). *Word Pictures in the New Testament* (Col 1:20). Broadman Press. https://ref.ly/logosres/LLS:46.50.2?off=3724506. Robertson notes that "the Apostle uses a rare word to describe reconciliation. His normal word is καταλλασσω [katallasso]. However, here he uses "this double compound (ἀπο, κατα [apo, kata] with ἀλλασσω [allasso]) occurs only here, verse 22, and Eph. 2:16, and nowhere else so far as known.... The addition of ἀπο [apo] here is clearly for the idea of **complete** reconciliation.... The use of τα παντα [ta panta] (all things, the universe) as if the universe were somehow out of harmony reminds us of the mystical passage in Rom. 8:19–23, which see for discussion. Sin somehow has put the universe out of joint. Christ will set it right. Unto himself (εἰς αὐτον [eis auton])." (emphasis is mine).

it also includes the removal of the offense which caused the disruption of peace and harmony. This was especially so in the relation of God with humanity, when Christ removed the enmity existing between God and mankind [humanity] by his vicarious sacrifice.[13]

When sin entered the human race, Adam turned his back on God. This rebellion continues today as it did with Adam. Why? Because of our relationship with Adam, the head of humanity. Reconciliation is the process whereby God in Christ turns us back to Himself! Note that Scripture never speaks about God being reconciled. He never changed! We, the people, need reconciliation! The Lord Jesus Christ is the Trinity's vehicle for completing our reconciliation.

Third, through Christ's sacrifice, God made peace through the blood of the cross. In Christ's substitutionary death in the place of sinners, God made peace available to those who place their faith in Christ. Those who trust Christ as Savior and Sin-bearer find the reality of peace they long for and desperately need.

Christ Himself offered peace to His followers. This concept is so fundamental that John 14:27 is worth repeating.

> **Peace** I leave with you, My **peace** I give to you; not as the world gives do I give to you. Let not your heart be troubled, neither let it be afraid (emphasis mine).

Jesus adds to this declaration in John 16:33.

---

13   Elwell, W. A., & Beitzel, B. J. (1988). Reconciliation. In *Baker Encyclopedia of the Bible* (Vol. 2, pp. 1823–1824). Baker Book House.

These things I have spoken to you, that in Me you may have **peace**. In the world, you will have tribulation, but be of good cheer, I have overcome the world (emphasis mine).

Not only can we enjoy peace amid troubles, but we know that in our Savior, we have an overwhelming Peacemaker!

When the gospel left its primarily Jewish roots and moved to a Gentile audience, Peter's message to Cornelius echoes the same theme in Acts 10:36-43.

The word which *God* sent to the children of Israel, preaching **peace** through Jesus Christ — He is Lord of all — that word you know, which was proclaimed throughout all Judea, and began from Galilee after the baptism which John preached: how God anointed Jesus of Nazareth with the Holy Spirit and with power, who went about doing good and healing all who were oppressed by the devil, for God was with Him. And we are witnesses of all things which He did both in the land of the Jews and in Jerusalem, whom they killed by hanging on a tree. Him God raised up on the third day and showed Him openly, not to all the people, but to witnesses chosen before by God, *even* to us who ate and drank with Him after He arose from the dead. And He commanded us to preach to the people and to testify that it is He who was ordained by God *to be* Judge of the living and the dead. To Him, all the prophets witness that, through His name, whoever believes in Him will receive remission of sins (emphasis mine).

God proclaimed the gospel of peace to Israel, the same gospel that came (and comes) to Gentiles. This movement started as a small kernel in Israel but now spreads to the ends of the earth.

The good news is that we can have peace with God through our Lord Jesus Christ! God makes this peace available to all those justified by faith in Christ.

> Therefore, having been justified by faith, we have peace with God through our Lord Jesus Christ. —Romans 5:1

If you have never trusted the Lord Jesus Christ as your Savior and Sin-Bearer, you can do so right now. You must recognize that you are a sinner separated from the God who loves you. Acknowledge your sin to God. Then, you must place your faith in Jesus Christ alone as your Savior. I did not know how to approach God properly when I trusted Christ. I prayed, "Lord Jesus, I know I am a sinner. I want you to forgive me. I trust you to be my Savior. I want you to change my life and make my life worth living." He did all that and much more.

My life changed forever! On March 28, 1969, I no longer wondered if I would go to heaven or hell. That night, when I placed my head on my pillow, I knew that if I died, I would awaken in heaven. Peace flooded my soul. That's what God promises!

Inner Peace

Not only does the Lord wish us to enjoy peace through justification, but He desires that we enjoy continued peace as we walk with Him. When people are genuinely born again (the Greek term can also mean "from above"), John 3:3, they possess the peace of God.

However, sanctification, growing in Christ-likeness, is essential for enjoying the full benefits of the peace found in Christ alone. These passages describe how to enjoy inner peace continuously.

Israel enjoyed seasons of peace and prosperity. In contrast to the promised blessings of the Palestinian Covenant (Deuteronomy 28-30), Israel, because of its persistent rebellion against God, currently lived on the precipice of ruin with the impending invasion of Babylon. In Isaiah the Lord offered them an olive branch.

> The work of righteousness will be **peace** and the effect of righteousness, quietness and assurance forever. —Isaiah 32:17

The Lord desires that we enjoy the fruit of righteousness, quietness and assurance forever. We don't always allow the Lord to work this out in our lives. I know many believers who do not exhibit God's peace. Beth and I have a friend who proudly declares, "It's my duty to worry. I cannot help myself." This person's declaration voids God's design for inner peace. Consequently, peace does not permeate this individual's life.

Once again, God loves you the way you are, but He's not content to leave you there! Allow Him to transform you into a vessel of peace.

In Isaiah, the Lord speaks of the blessedness of those who trust the Lord.

> You will keep *him* in perfect **peace**, *whose* mind *is* stayed *on You* because he trusts in You. —Isaiah 26:3

The Hebrew text reads *Shalom, Shalom,* which is translated as "perfect peace!" How wonderful to walk with unfettered trust in the Lord, which produces the fruit of inner peace. People pay counselors, psychologists, and psychiatrists big bucks to help them discover peace. The Lord offers, instead, Shalom, Shalom!

The Lord Jesus made the offer and freely dispenses peace to those who seek it. Isaiah 41:10 also reflects the reality of our confidence in our relationship with the Lord. The word "peace" does not occur in this passage, but the text oozes with the concept. In this context, the Lord rebukes those who worship idols and promises His faithful presence to those who walk in the midst of these hateful idolaters who seek to destroy Israel! The same principle applies to present-day believers as we walk in a strife-torn world.

> Fear not, for I *am* with you; Be not dismayed, for I *am* your God. I will strengthen you, yes, I will help you, I will uphold you with My righteous right hand. —Isaiah 41:10

A friend from one of the congregations we served bluntly stated, "God is not concerned with the small stuff in my life. He's only concerned with big stuff." My thought—does the Lord ever face "big stuff?" The Scripture declares His care for even the most minuscule detail. In Matthew 10:29-31, Jesus states that even a sparrow does not fall to the earth apart from the Father's will. There are no "big things" to God. He works even in the minutest details!

Psalm 85:8-10 shows the connection between experiencing peace as we walk with the Lord in contrast to the forfeited blessings that come when we seek to live independently of our Great King!

> I will listen to what God, the Lord, says.
> For he will make peace with his people,
> his faithful followers.

Yet they must not return to their foolish ways.
Certainly, his loyal followers will soon experience his
deliverance;
then his splendor will again appear in our land.
Loyal love and faithfulness meet;
deliverance and peace greet each other with a kiss.
(NET Bible)

Note that the theme seen in the other passages in this section repeats here. God will make peace with His people, His *faithful* followers. The Lord urges these believers not to "return to their foolish ways" (8). The text also tells us that loyal love (Hebrew, *hesed* חֶסֶד, a term that can mean "goodness, kindness, loyalty, lovingkindness"—a grace rooted in God's character) and faithfulness meet as a result of an authentic walk with the Lord. The last phrase tells us that "deliverance and peace greet each other with a kiss." Righteous living enjoys the blessing of God. Thus, the Lord urges us to walk faithfully in His ways so that we may enjoy the fruit of that walk, a life of peace!

Another passage in Isaiah demonstrates that inner peace (not salvation) may be forfeited when we make decisions without the Lord's blessing or direction. Consider the Lord's announcement to wayward Israel as they drifted from His care.

Oh, that you had heeded My commandments! Then your **peace** would have been like a river, and your righteousness like the waves of the sea (emphasis mine). —Isaiah 48:12

Had Israel honored the Lord by walking with Him, their peace would have flowed continually like a river, and their righteousness would have lapped their souls like the relentless waves of the sea.

Once again, it is easy to confuse salvation (justification) with sanctification. The Apostle John wrote the Gospel of John and 1 John. The purposes of John and 1 John are significantly different. The purpose of the Gospel of John is to introduce Jesus Christ as Savior and the salvation from sin found only in Him (John 20:30-31).

> And truly Jesus did many other signs in the presence of His disciples, which are not written in this book; but these are written that you may believe that Jesus is the Christ, the Son of God, and that believing you may have life in His name.

In 1 John, he desired to invite believers into the Apostolic fellowship that he and his fellow apostles enjoyed with the Father and the Son. " . . . that which we have seen and heard, we declare to you, that you also may have fellowship with us; and truly our fellowship is with the Father and with His Son Jesus Christ" (1 John 1:4).

One of the most famous passages from this book is 1 John 1:9: "If we confess our sins, He is faithful and just to forgive us our sins and to cleanse us from all unrighteousness." The text reflects the same theme found in the passages listed above. Sin causes a break in fellowship with God, not a loss of salvation. Fellowship is restored when we confess (agree with God) our sins. The result: God cleanses our sins and restores us to full fellowship. This text magnifies the grace of God as it applies to believers.

Many choose to take their own path and walk independently from the Lord. The result is the same. Rather than peace, restlessness and strife characterize their existence. These attitudes may be internal, but the effects of their choices almost always spill onto others in their circle. How tragic to see people rejecting God's offer of inner peace.

Here is a great example of the God of Peace flooding our souls with the Peace of God.

Mary Hutchison experienced a great deal of trauma early in her life. She was born with club feet. When she should be learning to walk, she endured broken bones every six weeks to straighten out her feet. The weight of the casts deformed her spine and created back problems she suffered for the balance of her life.

She lost her father when she was young. After she married, she birthed two sons and suffered her first miscarriage. Her husband abandoned her and her two young sons for a younger woman and never paid child support. This compound family fracture only added stress to her life. Mary worked two jobs to survive.

She later married Randy Hutchison, and they enjoyed 46 years of wedded bliss. God blessed them with the gift of a son, Michael, and she experienced a second miscarriage.

On Tuesday, December 7, 2021 (during COVID-19), Mary underwent a routine knee replacement surgery. Everything went as scheduled and expected. She planned to be discharged on Wednesday if she could pass all the requirements imposed by her physical therapist. The daytime nurse neglected to give Mary the pain pills that were scheduled for noon, and when the therapist came by shortly after 2:00, Mary was in a lot of pain and could not do everything necessary for the discharge. As a result, she needed to remain in the hospital an additional night. When Randy left Wednesday evening, the doctors and nurses removed all the monitors and assured them that everything was progressing on schedule.

When the phone rang shortly before 5:00 a.m. on December 9, Randy anticipated the caller would announce that Mary was ready to be discharged. The doctor on the line said, "The nurse checked her at midnight, and she was fine. At 2:00, she checked her, and she was sleeping, so the nurse did not awaken her. When she checked at 4:00 a.m., she was not responsive. We did everything we could, but your wife is dead."

Randy, known for his fiery disposition, became furious. "My anger boiled up as I thought about the inept day shift nurse, the 2-hour checks at night, no monitors on her and the doctor's great way of informing me."

He drove angrily to the hospital. All he could think about was grabbing the doctor by the throat. Randy was not in a good frame of mind, to say the least.

"When I got to the hospital, I was stopped at the door and told that I could not enter until visiting hours. I told the guard that she better call the cops now because I had just had a call that my wife was dead and that I WAS going to see her. She stepped aside. When I got upstairs, a nurse informed me that the doctor wasn't there, but I could speak to a hospitalist on duty. He took me to the room. When I went in and saw her, she still had a breathing tube in her mouth from the resuscitation attempt. I picked up her hand and kissed her on the forehead. I looked at her face, and she looked very peaceful. The first thought that came to my mind was, 'Why did God take her?' Then I realized that she was with Jesus, and there was no more pain or worry. I also thought about her meeting her two other children and seeing her father again. I realized that He had just blessed her, and I should be feeling joy for her. All the anger just melted away."[14]

It's natural for a person to be angry at a time like this. In this case, anger with the nurse, with the doctor and with the hospital. But,

---

14   Randy Hutchison, personal conversation, July 30, 2023, used by permission.

by the grace of God, Randy experienced supernatural peace—a peace that only comes from the God of peace, Who gives His followers the Peace of God.

This is not to say that Randy doesn't miss Mary. He misses her terribly. But comfort returns when Randy remembers the assurance of the promise given to Christ-followers, "To be absent from the body is to be present with the Lord" (2 Corinthians 5:8).

A pastor friend is fond of saying, "God's got all the things!" He does! Enjoy the peace He provides—a peace that passes understanding!

Points to Ponder

1. Can you think of times when you chose to live life according to your desires? Did you sense that you forfeited the peace of God in the process?

2. How did you respond when you discovered a lack of peace?

3. If you have unconfessed sin, now is a great time to apply 1 John 1:9 to your Christian walk.

If you continue to live in a place of rebellion, now is the time to seek restoration. I've never known one person who responded positively to the overtures of God to return to fellowship who regretted that decision. But I know others who chose not to return. Their lives continued to be marked by restlessness and turmoil. Please return. The Lord is waiting!

Peace with One Another

In the Peanuts cartoon strip, Linus Van Pelt declared, "I love mankind [humanity]; it's people I can't stand!" This quote hits home. We all struggle with people who live in our space and time. Conflict is inevitable. However, the Word of God has much to say regarding Christ-followers dwelling together in unity. Here is a sequence of topics that proves challenging. However, the Lord, in His infinite wisdom, offers us heavenly solutions to our common struggles.

- *Dwelling Together in Unity*
- *Exercising Christian Liberty*
- *Ethnic Unity*
- *Humility*
- *Rulership of Peace*

Dwelling Together in Unity

God designed us for healthy relationships. From the very beginning of creation, God said, "It is not good for man to be alone. I will make him a helper comparable to him" (Genesis 2:18). This statement referred to Eve. This pattern recurs in the Old Testament and the early days of the church as people assembled for growth and ministry. Here is some wisdom from the Psalms.

> Behold, how good and how pleasant *it is* for brethren to dwell together in unity! —Psalm 133:1

I believe we can all say "Amen" to this statement. We all know some folks who love to live in the swamp of conflict, but I am thankful these are few and far between. Serving with people who know how to love and get along satisfies!

I served four churches as their full-time pastor and as an interim in four additional churches. Two of the four full-time churches were a joy with great, but not perfect, harmony, and two offered great challenges. Unfortunately, too often, I created or added to the challenges!

Points to Ponder

1. Do you struggle to dwell with others in unity, especially if they think differently from you?

2. What attitudes or actions do you need to implement to dwell in unity?

Exercising Christian Liberty

God gave us a number of black-and-white issues that we must observe. However, we face a plethora of gray areas in our Christian walk that are neither black nor white. These gray areas far outnumber God's concrete demands. These can include what Bible translation we should use, issues of dress (so long as it is modest), where we send our children to school: home, parochial or public. Romans 14-15 and 1 Corinthians 8-10 outline how we must exercise our Christian liberty.

Problems arise when believers make "law" when God does not. We must learn to walk in Christian charity in these areas.

> Therefore, do not let your good be spoken of as evil, for the kingdom of God is not eating and drinking, but righteousness and peace and joy in the Holy Spirit. For he who serves

Christ in these things *is* acceptable to God and approved by men. Therefore, let us pursue the things *which make* for peace and the things by which one may edify another.
—Romans 14:16-19

The following is attributed to Augustine, Bishop of Hippo, North Africa.

In essentials, unity; in non-essentials, liberty; in all things, charity.

This statement fits with the tenor of Romans 14-15 and 1 Corinthians 8-10. Unfortunately, many Pharisaic Christians heap all kinds of guilt on people who do not follow their personal dictates. I frequently deal with situations where people don't understand the principles of Christian Liberty. It's tragic to take out our dustpan and whisk broom to sweep up the carnage of legalistic practice. Church body parts litter the floor after Mr. Dominating Pharisee, or Subtle Susie finishes "polishing" a church. Without question, we must hold the fundamentals of the faith. However, there is a great deal more "gray" area in following Christ than following self-imposed Pharisaical absolutes!

Remember the Pharisees demanding proper washing and etiquette. Jesus dashed their dogmatic desires when He "conspired" with sinners and tax collectors. For He, indeed, was about pursuing righteousness, peace and joy in the Holy Spirit. That, my friends, is attractive to those seeking a relationship with the Savior, not regaling grating, dogmatic rules.

I've enjoyed serving in several countries as I train pastors, missionaries, Christian workers and the trainers of pastors. Cultures vary widely. In one country, custom required us to stand and pray before each meal. That was new to me. What did I do? My freedom-loving mind screamed, "Pray sitting down!" because I disdain rules that impose on my freedom (I'm that kind of rebel). What did I do? I stood to pray before meals. Cultural mores should not dictate our actions. However, this was not a hill to die on. The peace of Christ is of more excellent value than our personal preferences. It is a joy to dwell in unity!

Points to Ponder

1. Do you have any "hobby horses" you wish to ride that are not biblical but culturally or deeply ingrained in your thinking? You "know they are right" when they are not?

2. Spend a great deal of time in Romans 14-15 and 1 Corinthians 8-10 to sharpen your focus on the "essentials" while giving grace in the non-essentials.

3. Ask God for grace when dealing with gray areas.

Ethnic Unity

In Ephesians 2, the Apostle tells us about the great unity the Lord provides for His church body, a fellowship comprised of Jews and Gentiles. Christ is our peace, not our pedigree! We all come from the seed of Adam and need the touch of the Savior. As our peace, He joins enemies together in harmony. Once again, we see the term reconciliation. Here, the text tells us that Christ has reconciled the two natural enemies into one body through the cross (Greek, *dia,* translated "through" indicates "of means, or agency"). This cross purchased our unity. In this peacemaking process, Jesus transports those near (Jews) and those far (Gentiles) into one body. This concept, especially in today's ethnic divide, is essential.

> For He Himself is our **peace**, who has made both one and has broken down the middle wall of separation, having abolished in His flesh the enmity, *that is,* the law of commandments *contained* in ordinances, so as to create in Himself one new man *from* the two, *thus* making **peace**, and that He might reconcile them both to God in one body through the cross, thereby putting to death the enmity.
> And He came and preached **peace** to you who were afar off and to those who were near. —Ephesians 2:14-17

A remarkable backstory: I first traveled to Singapore Bible College (SBC) in 2017 to teach a Doctor of Ministries course on Church Revitalization. We had a section in our training dedicated to conflict resolution and biblical peacemaking. During this segment, I had each student share a painful reminder from the past. The class of sixteen included five students from Sri Lanka. The Sri Lankan population is composed primarily of two main ethnic groups: the indigenous majority Sinhalese and the minority Tamils who migrated to Sri Lanka from India. In 1983, these two ethnic groups became embroiled in a bitter civil war that lasted 26 years and resulted in the deaths of some 60,000 to 100,000 people. The flash point of the Civil War occurred when Tamil separatists, known as the Liberation Tigers of Tamil Eelam (LTTE), ambushed and killed twelve Sinhalese soldiers and an officer in the northern part of the country (Tamil territory). In retaliation, some Sinhalese in the capital city of Colombo attacked Tamils, where 5,638 Tamils were massacred, and another 250,000 fled to the north.[15]

In my class, Anthony C., Tamil by birth, stated that he lived in Trincomalee, a city on the east coast of Sri Lanka, when the civil war started. Hostile Sinhalese soldiers burned his home. He lost all his possessions as he fled for his life. A Sinhalese general gave Anthony refuge, showed him kindness, and helped him return to the relative safety of the north of Sri Lanka. For many years, the pain of this encounter burned into his soul. He could not forgive those who had taken everything from him. Then he met Christ, and the fever of revenge left him, and the love and forgiveness found only in Christ flooded his heart.

The Encounter: As we went around the class, we came to Devapriya H. He said, "I am Sinhalese. I was one of the soldiers (sailors) who threw Molotov cocktails into Tamil homes in 1983. I may be the one who set your home on fire." The classroom grew very quiet. Everyone waited with bated breath to see what was going to happen. I looked at Dr. Rick Griffith, the D.Min. director for SBC, and he looked at me. I whispered, "Did I just hear what I thought I heard?" He shook his head in amazement, shrugged his shoulders and remained speechless! No human being could have orchestrated this classroom encounter! No one in the class knew this exchange would take place. This event was a God Moment!

This was my final day of class, so we all drove to a restaurant downtown for lunch. As it happened, these two men rode with Rick and me and sat next to each other in the back seat while Rick and I rode up front. I turned and asked both men questions

---

15   https://en.wikipedia.org/wiki/Sri_Lankan_Civil_War, accessed 6/19/2023. These facts correspond with the account given in class by the two students.

about their hearts and feelings. Both said, "The past no longer matters. We are now brothers in Christ. The Lord Jesus removed the burning hatred we both shared in 1983. We are different men now. We are brothers in Christ!" Divapira writes, "Now we are serving with and respecting each other in the same faculty at Lanka Bible College and Seminary."[16]

This encounter is a living example of the Lord breaking down barriers between people groups. In this case, the divisions included ethnic, cultural and ideological differences coupled with deep bitterness. How is reconciliation possible in these scenarios? The Lord Jesus breaks down the walls of separation—not only for Jews and Gentiles but for Sinhalese and Tamils. He also works among multitudes of others who face bitter enmity—a work so needed in today's world.

What can we say about these types of encounters? Hallelujah! Only Christ produces peace where there is no peace! Where do you need the Lord to work in you?

Points to Ponder

1. Do you struggle with ethnic, cultural or ideological differences in your relationships?

2. Where do you need the Lord to change you?

---

16   Personal email correspondence, June 22-26, 2023. Used by permission. Unfortunately, Charles H. suffered a stroke prior to this correspondence and could not reply.

Humility

Someone once quipped, "Pride is the only disease known to man that makes everyone sick except the one who has it." Here are some passages that encourage people to walk with humility.

> But He gives more grace. Therefore, He says: "God resists the proud, but gives grace to the humble." —James 4:6

> Likewise, you younger people, submit yourselves to your elders. Yes, all of you, be submissive to one another and be clothed with humility, for God resists the proud but gives grace to the humble. —1 Peter 5:5

> Pride goes before destruction, and a haughty spirit before a fall. —Proverbs 16:18

In commenting on this concept found in Proverbs 16, the following appeared in *Reader's Digest*. "The problem with patting yourself on the back is that your hands aren't free to break your fall."[17]

The next passage does not use the word "humility." However, it clearly states the concept and demonstrates how essential humility is as we attempt to preserve the Spirit-established unity in the Body of Christ.

> I, therefore, the prisoner of the Lord, beseech you to walk worthy of the calling with which you were called, with all lowliness and gentleness, with longsuffering, bearing with one another in love, endeavoring to keep the unity of the Spirit in the bond of peace. —Ephesians 4:1-3

---

17   *Reader's Digest*, December 1998, p 172, quoting a *Newsweek* article.

Since the Spirit already establishes unity, the Lord urges us to endeavor to maintain that unity. We must work at it. This is only possible in the Lord's strength. Woe to those who disrupt the Body of Christ (see also Titus 3:9-11, Matthew 18:15-18, Romans 16:17-18 and 3 John 9-10).

Rulership of Peace

Once again, the Lord challenges us to allow God's peace to reign in our hearts. Is that possible? Absolutely. As the peace of God rules and we apply the Word of God to living, we will enjoy a fruitful time with one another.

> And let the **peace of God** rule in your hearts, to which also you were called in one body; and be thankful. Let the word of Christ dwell in you richly in all wisdom, teaching and admonishing one another in psalms and hymns and spiritual songs, singing with grace in your hearts to the Lord (emphasis mine). —Colossians 3:15-16

As outlined in Colossians 3:15-22, this peace impacts the church body (3:16), marriage (3:18-19), children and parents (3:20-21) and even slaves and masters (though today, these statements more reflect the relationships between employers and employees (3:22)).

Years ago, I heard an account about a man who stood up in an open-air meeting and began to sing the doxology in the middle of the preacher's message. People asked him to stop interrupting. He stated, "I cannot help but sing. For you see, I was an alcoholic. I lost everything: my possessions, my dignity, and I nearly lost my family. Then I met the Lord. He turned hate into love. He turned alcohol into furniture. He turned my wife back to me. And now, my children are no longer afraid to claim me as their father. Yes! Praise God from whom all blessings flow!" Only God can produce this rulership of peace in us that spills over onto all around us.

Points to Ponder

1. Do you struggle with any of these five areas of peace we just discussed?

2. If so, how should you respond to the Lord and to others with whom you struggle?

Peace with Our Enemies

Worldwide Pictures produced a movie after a Billy Graham crusade in Denver called "For Pete's Sake." It featured a new believer named Pete, who responded to the invitation to trust Christ at the crusade. I was a new Christ follower when I saw the film, but it made an impression. First, it was filmed in Colorado (my home state), which piqued my interest, but I identified with Pete and his not-very-sanctified walk with the Lord. In one scene, he comes home from the tree nursery with his arms loaded with roses equipped with particularly nasty thorns. I'm reconstructing the conversation from memory. As he walked in the door, he said to his wife, "Honey, I'll bet these babies will fix our neighbor. If he runs over our rose garden one more time with these roses, that will be the last time! These thorns will flatten his tires." Another well-dressed gentleman appeared in the background. Pete's wife said, "I would like to introduce you to

Pastor Smith (I don't remember his name). He is here to discuss our decision to follow Christ at the crusade." Ouch! I remember a long, awkward silence in the film.

Many of us can relate to Pete. We live in a dog-eat-dog world. When wronged, we desire to get even. Some will even lie awake at night trying to think of ways to strike back at people who treat them poorly. I know I have.

What did Jesus have to say about our enemies? Here's His take from the Sermon on the Mount.

> You have heard that it was said, 'You shall love your neighbor and hate your enemy.' But I say to you, love your enemies, bless those who curse you, do good to those who hate you, and pray for those who spitefully use you and persecute you, that you may be sons of your Father in heaven, for He makes His sun rise on the evil and on the good, and sends rain on the just and on the unjust. For if you love those who love you, what reward have you? Do not even the tax collectors do the same? And if you greet your brethren only, what do you do more *than others?* Do not even the tax collectors do so? Therefore, you shall be perfect, just as your Father in heaven is perfect. —Matthew 5:43-48

Now, instead of lying awake at night plotting my revenge, I lie awake trying to determine how I can bless my enemies. That's an increasingly pleasant task.

Here's another passage that outlines a believer's response to their enemy.

Repay no one evil for evil. Have regard for good things in the sight of all men. If it is possible, as much as depends on you, live peaceably with all men. Beloved, do not avenge yourselves, but *rather* give place to wrath; for it is written, "Vengeance *is* Mine, I will repay," says the Lord. Therefore, "If your enemy is hungry, feed him; If he is thirsty, give him a drink; For in so doing you will heap coals of fire on his head." Do not be overcome by evil, but overcome evil with good. —Romans 12:17-21

The Lord lays out several essential steps for believers to follow when dealing with difficult people.

- Do not repay evil for evil. Doing so will only escalate an already difficult situation. Our friend Pete had yet to learn this lesson.

- As much as depends on you, live peaceably with all men. We cannot control the actions of others, but the Lord asks us to do our part to produce harmony.

- Vengeance is God's business, not ours. Think of Martyr Stephen in Acts 7:60, where he, like the Lord Jesus (Luke 23:34), asked the Lord not to charge his tormentors with sin. One member of his "audience" was the future Apostle Paul. I've often wondered how Stephen's deportment impacted Saul of Tarsus.

- By treating an enemy with kindness, you will heap coals of fire on his head. Some think our actions will make hell hotter for this individual. However, another view seems more prudent. In so doing, pangs of contrition will more likely fall on the turbulent sinner.[18]

---

18   Witmer, J. A. (1985). Romans. In J. F. Walvoord & R. B. Zuck (Eds.), *The Bible Knowledge Commentary: An Exposition of the Scriptures* (Vol. 2, p. 490). Victor Books. https://ref.ly/logosres/LLS:29.1.1?off=8225703. Paul rejected revenge as a Christian response to injustice, "do not avenge

A multitude of illustrations come to mind. Here's an account from the professional baseball world.

> Former Boston Red Sox third baseman Wade Boggs hated going to Yankee Stadium, not because of the Yankees, but because of a fan. The guy had a seat close to the field, and when the Red Sox were in town, he would torment Boggs by shouting obscenities and insults.
>
> One day, Boggs decided he'd had enough. He walked directly over to the man and said, "Hey, fella, are you the guy who is always yelling at me?" The man said, "Yeah, it's me. What are you going to do about it?"
>
> Wade took a new baseball out of his pocket, autographed it, tossed it to the man, and returned to the field to continue his pre-game routine. The man never yelled at Boggs again; he became one of Wade's biggest fans at Yankee Stadium.[19]

Here is one of my many personal failures. During my first pastorate in Southeast Dallas, someone broke into Grove Haven Baptist Church, the church I served. The church was in a changing neighborhood with a growing crime rate. I purposefully asked our Sunday School teachers and leaders to ensure they never left money in the church building. One Sunday evening, someone broke into the church and found about $1.14 in Aunt John's Sunday School room. Nothing else turned up missing, and damage was minimal.

---

yourselves." Did he then imply another kind of revenge when he spoke of heaping coals on their head (perhaps an image of hell)? No! "Do not be overcome by evil, but overcome evil with good." The burning coals may refer to an Egyptian ritual during which one demonstrated genuine repentance by carrying hot coals in some container. These words are in concert with Jesus' admonition in Matthew 5:43-47, "Bless those who curse you, do good to those who hat e you .. that you may be sons of your Father in heaven."

19   Don Chisholm in *Pulpit Helps*, AMG International, October 1999.

However, the next Sunday, we locked every window and door. It would be difficult for anyone to break in. When I walked into the building on Monday, it was really hot. When I entered the kitchen, the burners on the gas range were burning full tilt. Intruders broke a window in the breezeway between the auditorium and the educational wing and made their way through the building. When they found no money, they stacked paper towels and napkins on the gas range, turned the burners on high and left the building. Ashes drifted into the trash can beside the stove, but the paper didn't ignite.

I called the police department, and some officers arrived. When the burglar(s) broke a window, he cut himself, and blood covered the broken glass, along with many fingerprints and palm prints. I thought they would nail this burglar. There's plenty of evidence!

I stood outside as the officers completed their work. I was angry. So, I said, "I would like to grab whoever did this by the lapel and shake some sense into them." The officer rejoined, "Doesn't the Bible say, 'Vengeance is mine, I will repay.'?" (I'm sure this officer had waited years to say this to a pastor!). I sheepishly replied, "Yeah, I think it says that somewhere." I knew exactly where—Romans 12. Nailed! I felt about an inch tall!

Now, in all fairness, I did not desire to exact revenge. I just wanted the perpetrator to think about the seriousness of his actions. He would experience "Shaken Sinner Syndrome." Fortunately, the building did not burn to the ground, and the damage was minimal. I refrained from taking vengeance. Most importantly, the police officer humbled me. The Lord drove home His point about taking revenge!

Another potent passage relates to God's desire for us to live at peace with our enemies.

Pursue **peace** with all *people* and holiness, without which no one will see the Lord: looking carefully lest anyone fall short of the grace of God; lest any root of bitterness springing up cause trouble, and by this, many become defiled. —Hebrews 12:13-14

I see this root of bitterness thriving in deeply conflicted churches! Bitterness and anxiety overrun these fellowships. The tragic result: The Name of Christ is discredited because of self-will and bitterness. In their bitterness, church members drag the name of Christ through the gutters. Tragic.

Years ago, I heard an account of a missionary family who purchased some nice dining room furniture for a great price. The person they hired to finish the furniture did not meet the wife's expectations. She was hot. "I'm going back there to get this straightened out. The guy did a terrible job. I'll give him a piece of my mind."

The husband reminded her, "Just remember that when you finish with him, my job is to try to win him to the Lord."

Does bitterness fuel you? Vengeful thoughts and bitterness almost seem to be the lingua franca of the day. Once again, Christ-followers should live to a different, higher standard. Prof Hendricks at Dallas Seminary used to say the following about those who respond in anger. "He gave him a piece of his mind that he could ill afford to lose!" Let's allow the Spirit of God to check our spirit before we speak. James reminds us, "Let every man be swift to hear, slow to speak, slow to wrath" (James 1:19). Sage advice in a world filled with anger!

Points to Ponder

1. Do you struggle with feelings of bitterness or resentment towards others, especially toward those who treat you poorly?

2. Do you need an attitude adjustment?

3. If you responded with vengeance, what was the outcome?

CHAPTER 4

CONFLICT EXPLORED

Conflict Defined and Five Types of Conflict
- **Conflict Defined**
- **Conflict with God**
- **Self-Condemnation**
- **Spiritual Warfare**
- **Interpersonal Conflict**
- **Conflict with Our Enemies**

Conflict surrounds us like water surrounds a fish. We are so immersed in difficulties that we fail to comprehend our surroundings! In this section, we want to define conflict and examine five different conflict arenas: Conflict with God, Self-Condemnation, Spiritual Warfare, Interpersonal Conflict and Conflict with our Enemies. These closely align with the four areas discussed concerning The Peace of God. Because of these five types of conflict, we need the Peace of God to rule and overrule in our lives!

Here are two realities we face. First, conflict is inevitable and these are some stark realities we must understand.

- The history of the world is the history of conflict.
- Spiritual Conflict: Human history is the history of the conflict between Satan, God and humanity.
- All conflict can be traced back to spiritual conflict.

However, Christ desires that "they [Christ-followers] may be one, just as you, Father, are in me and I in you" (John 17:21). This reality can only occur through the power of the Spirit working in us! Consequently, we will always need to be aware of the atmosphere surrounding us and constantly pursue the need for peacemaking.

Second, conflict is universal and impacts everyone. Even great leaders of the faith struggled with conflict. Here are a few passages that show the permeating presence of conflict.

Abram and Lot over grazing rights	Genesis 13:5-11
Twelve tribes over "rival" altar	Joshua 22
Saul and David	1 Samuel 16-31
Some of the Apostles doubted Jesus' resurrection	Matthew 28:2-28
Conflict over language and culture	Acts 6:1-7
Paul and Barnabas over mission and vision	Acts 15:35-41
Peter and Paul over kosher practices	Galatians 2:11-21
Deep divisions in the church in Corinth	1 Corinthians 1:12-13

This conflict list can go on and on, chapter by chapter, throughout the Scriptures.

If conflict rocked these pillars of the faith, might it occasionally visit our churches, homes or businesses? I repeat my conviction. Conflict is inevitable. Thus, pastors and leaders must learn how to handle the battles that are certain to break out in their spheres of influence, whether in churches, homes, businesses, civic organizations and the like.

Conflict Defined

In *Pastor Unique*, I define conflict as "a difference of opinion over mission, vision and values that frustrates a person's goals or desires."[20] Here I would like to add "purposes" to the list. As I work with deeply conflicted individuals, groups, business leaders and churches, I see differences in mission, vision, values and *purposes* at the core of many of these conflict issues.

After we married, Beth and I became involved in First Baptist Church, Fort Collins, Colorado. A young man who grew up as a missionary kid in Japan moved back to Fort Collins. He and his wife were outfitting a property up the Buckhorn Canyon west of Fort Collins as a Christian camp and retreat center. Our Sunday School class scheduled a Saturday workday to help with roofing, cleaning and clearing clutter. Several of the ladies took over organizing meals for the day. Their decisiveness ran afoul of other ladies who felt they lost their voice in the planning process. My question: Did it matter? Apparently, it did. A potential firestorm smoldered just below the surface. This unrest badly damaged relationships—relationships to this day that bear the

20   Lavern E. Brown, Gordon E. Penfold, and Gary J. Westra, *Pastor Unique: Becoming a Turnaround Leader* (Bloomington, IN, Westbow Press, 2016) 154.

scars of needless harshness. The game of one-upmanship (I'm more valuable than you, and my contributions are more valuable than yours) cuts relationships to the core. Folks, for the most part, did not resolve these issues. Tension still exists when these couples see each other forty-plus years later. How unfortunate.

Conflict with God

When I think of Conflict with God, I immediately think of God's disfavor with humanity. However, conflict with God is a two-way street. Certainly, the Lord has issues with us, the progeny of Adam. However, the children of Adam often find themselves upset with the Lord God. We will look at both scenarios.

- *God's Conflict with Humanity*
- *Humanity's Conflict with God*

God's Conflict with Humanity

The conflict between God and humanity weaves its way through the warp and woof of Scripture. After their fall, Adam and Eve hid from God and feared his presence because they knew they disobeyed His direct commandment. The intimate fellowship enjoyed by the first couple and their creator suffered a great schism that only the Lord Jesus Christ can bridge. This conflict between God and people expanded in the exchange between Cain and the Lord when the Lord did not respect Cain and his offering (Genesis 4:4-5). Hebrews 11:4 states that Abel offered his sacrifice by faith, but Cain did not. Cain acted out his displeasure by murdering his brother (Genesis 4:8).

Later in Genesis 6:3, after the continued expansion of sinful behavior and practices, we read, "And the LORD said, 'My Spirit
shall not strive[21] with man forever, for he *is* indeed flesh; yet his
days shall be one hundred and twenty years.'"

Zechariah 1:2 plainly states, "The Lord has been very angry
with your fathers." The Lord God became fed up with Israel's
stubborn rebelliousness and wanton disregard for the law he
instituted. After demonstrating great patience with the wayward nation, the Lord acted decisively. Assyria carried Israel's
Northern Kingdom captive in 722 BC and Judah with three
waves of deportation spearheaded by Nebuchadnezzar, the
Babylonian king between 605 and 586 BC. (Even in discipline,
the Lord graciously promised restoration, a promise that awaits
ultimate fulfillment with the second coming of Christ.)

God declares His issues with humanity and the Jewish nation
in many biblical passages. These Old Testament passages use
the verb strive (Hebrew *ryb* רִבִי, quarrel; conduct a legal suit).
For example, in Isaiah 57:16, the Lord declares his position. "For
I will not **contend** forever, nor will I always be angry; For the
spirit would fail before Me, And the souls *which* I have made"
(emphasis mine). Note: the Lord does not wish to "wear us out."
Psalm 103:19, Jeremiah 25:31 and Hosea 4:1 further state God's
displeasure with Israel. These passages forcefully demonstrate
that God will deal with insubordination and defiance! See also
Isaiah 3:13, Jeremiah 2:9, Hosea 12:2 and Micah 6:1-2.

---

21   Biblical Studies Press. (2005). *The NET Bible First Edition; Bible. English. NET Bible.; The NET
Bible*. Biblical Studies Press. NET Bible translator's note, Genesis 6:3.The Hebrew term translated
"strive" is וְלֹדִי (yadon), a Qal imperfect tense. It can be translated as "strive" or "dwell with."
This word is used twice in the OT; here and in Nehemiah 3:7 (as a name). "The verb form וֹדִי
only occurs here. Some derive it from the verbal root דִי (din, "to judge") and translate "strive"
or "contend with" (so NIV), but in this case one expects the form to be יָדִין (yadin). The Old
Greek has "remain with," a rendering which may find support from an Arabic cognate (see C.
Westermann, Genesis, 1:375). (Net Bible note). So whether it should be translated as "strive" or
abide with (protect), the point is clear. Regardless of the translation, the Lord takes issue with
humanity. The flood followed shortly on the heels of this pronouncement.

Other passages found below show God's contention and displeasure with Israel, humanity, and the nations without the use of *ryb*.

- Hear, all you peoples! Listen, O earth, and all that is in it! Let the Lord GOD be a witness against you, The Lord from His holy temple. For behold, the LORD is coming out of His place; He will come down and tread on the high places of the earth. The mountains will melt under Him, and the valleys will split like wax before the fire, like waters poured down a steep place (Micah 1:2-4).

- For we know Him who said, "Vengeance is Mine, I will repay," says the Lord. And again, "The LORD will judge His people." It is a fearful thing to fall into the hands of the living God (Hebrews 10:30-31).

- Then he fell to the ground and heard a voice saying to him, "Saul, Saul, why are you persecuting Me?" And he said, "Who are You, Lord?" Then the Lord said, "I am Jesus, whom you are persecuting. It *is* hard for you to kick against the goads." Acts 9:4-5. Here, we see Saul of Tarsus struggling against the Lord's plan for him.

- The messages to the seven churches of Revelation 2-3 show the Lord's displeasure with His church leaders. For example, in Revelation 2:4, the Lord Jesus takes issue with the messenger (Gk *aggelos)* pastor of the church in Ephesus (I understand the "messenger" to refer to the pastor.)[22] The Lord emphatically states, "I

---

22   The following description of the meaning of *aggelos* is taken from Aubrey Malphurs and Gordon E. Penfold, *Re:Vision: The Key to Transforming Your Church* (Grand Rapids, Baker, 2014), Endnote 17, 270. "There is debate as to the identity of the seven angels. The debate focuses on the meaning of the term *aggelos*. The question is whether the *aggelos* are angels or messengers, that is, the pastors. The view chosen greatly impacts the meaning of the passage. The term *aggelos* is defined in the following two ways. One is human messengers: an envoy, one who is sent by men or by God. The other is supernatural powers, such angels as messengers of God (Walter Bauer, F. Wilbur Gingrich, William F. Arndt, and Frederick W. Danker, *A Greek-English Lexicon of the New Testament and Other Early Christian Literature*, 2nd ed. [Chicago: University of Chicago Press], s.v. *aggelos*)."

have this against you, that you have left your first love."
He also speaks forcefully to the messenger at Pergamos,
Thyatira, Sardis and Laodicea.

These passages demonstrate how the Lord interacts with individuals, people groups and nations as He directs their steps toward a deeper and more satisfying relationship with Him. He also shows His restraint, allowing people to withstand His leadership and lordship.

Such is the God of Grace who permits people to either submit or rebel against his leadership. Matthew 23:37-39 illustrates this truth. The Lord longed for repentance among the people of Israel. Listen to the Lord Jesus' plaintive cry to a people with hardened hearts.

> O Jerusalem, Jerusalem, the one who kills the prophets and stones those who are sent to her! How often I wanted to gather your children together, as a hen gathers her chicks under *her* wings, but you were not willing! See! Your house is left to you desolate. For I say to you, you shall see Me no more till you say, *"Blessed is He who comes in the name of the Lord!"*

Even in the distress of the present, the Lord offers them grace and hope for the future! Such is the nature of our Great God!

When I first heard the gospel in 1969, I understood God's displeasure with my sin and that he had a serious issue with me! That realization propelled me towards a new relationship with Christ. I'm thankful for this truth!

Points to Ponder

1. Do you find yourself resisting God's overtures to you?

2. Do you demonstrate active rebellion against God? If so, what is the rebellion, and how must you respond to that rebellion?

Humanity's Conflict with God

Not only does God contend with people, but people also contend with God. Isaiah 45:9 says, "Woe to him who **strives** with his Maker! *Let* the potsherd *strive* with the potsherds of the earth! Shall the clay say to him who forms it, 'What are you making?' Or shall your handiwork *say,* 'He has no hands'?" Additionally, Israel contended at the waters of Merebah (a name derived from *ryb)* in Numbers 20:13.

Think of Jonah and his selfish ambitions. He did not like the grace and mercy of God extended to the enemies of Israel (Jonah 4:2). He became angry when his "shade plant" withered. The Lord asked Jonah, "Is it right for you to be angry about the plant?" And he said, "It is for me to be angry, even to death." Talk about a contentious attitude against the Lord! Then, the Lord unveiled his compassion for Nineveh. It was far greater than Jonah's compassion for his plant.

Many passages deal with Israel's disobedience to the Lord and His prophets. Indeed, people become angry and rebellious when they do not get their way. Some prophets even lost their lives to angry mobs, murdered because of Israel's unwillingness to surrender to the Lord's direction.

I recently spoke with a man at a community gathering. He said, "My sister was ill. I prayed for her recovery. She died. God didn't answer my prayer. I'm not going to seek him any further." This kind of anger with God is the theme we repeatedly see in the Old and New Testaments. God didn't do what I wanted Him to do, so I'm angry. Once again, as Isaiah 45:9 states, it's a dangerous game to strive with your Maker!

Contentious attitudes impact me as well. Here is one event from my life. Beth and I went for a long walk one evening during my second pastorate. I am generally quite talkative, but not that evening. I walked in uncomfortable silence. After about thirty minutes, I asked, "Beth, what's wrong with me?" She responded, "I don't know, but I wish you would figure it out because you're killing me." We continued to walk for another thirty minutes in silence. I finally said, " I know what's wrong with me. I am angry with God. I have a vision of the direction the church needs to go. I've prayed about it and want to see it come to pass, but it's not happening. That's why I'm angry."

I'm not alone in this. Habakkuk was upset with the state of Israel. He inquired of God, and the Lord responded, "I'm going to show you what's going to happen. I'm going to bring the Chaldeans in here, and they're going to wipe Israel off the map. That's what I'm going to do" (my paraphrase of Habakkuk 1:2-11).

Habakkuk grew dismayed at the Lord's response. I'm para-phrasing here. "Lord, you're going to do what? Don't you know how ruthless the Chaldeans are? They are far worse than Israel." Habakkuk then cried out to the Lord and said, "You are of purer eyes than to behold evil and cannot look on wickedness" (Habakkuk 1:13a).

Habakkuk finally reached a moment of peace. He said, "O LORD, I have heard Your speech and was afraid; O LORD, revive Your work in the midst of the years! In the midst of the years make it known; In wrath remember mercy" (Habakkuk 3:2). When Habakkuk recognized these truths, he reached a point of surrender while asking for a future transformation of Israel. We can learn much from this prophet.

King David became angry with God when he attempted to bring the Ark of the Covenant into Jerusalem on an ox cart. David had the right heart in transporting the ark, just the wrong method. The priests were responsible for bearing the Ark, not an ox cart. David did it "his way." When Uzzah stuck out his hand to steady the Ark, the Lord struck Uzzah down. We find David's response in 2 Samuel 6:8. "And David became angry because of the LORD's outbreak against Uzzah, and he called the name of the place Perez Uzzah (outbreak against Uzzah) to this day."

In Psalm 73, Asaph said, "Truly God *is* good to Israel, to such as are pure in heart. But as for me, my feet had almost stumbled; my steps had nearly slipped, for I *was* envious of the boastful when I saw the prosperity of the wicked" (Psalm 73:1-3). Asaph's complaint rose to God because He felt God was unfair to the righteous who suffered while the wicked prospered. This issue is an age-old dilemma. As a result, Asaph was angry with God.

Contrast his initial attitude with Psalm 73:17. Asaph said, "When I sought to understand this, it was too painful for me—until I went into the sanctuary of God. Then I understood their end."

Asaph needed some eternal perspective. That must happen to us. We must gain eternal perspective when we get angry and upset with God. We see this reality throughout Scripture! Humanity experiences conflict with God, and we need to gain eternal perspective to understand and deal with our dissatisfaction. In addition, we need to deepen our understanding of the Lord and His work.

I've discovered it is not good to be angry with God. I finally realized that God is not at my beck and call to do what I want. I need to align myself with His desires. His designs for life far exceed my pitiful plans!

Now, when I get angry, I pause and ask myself, "Why am I angry? Why am I so upset?" Normally, I try to squeeze God into my mold rather than shape myself after Him. My plans are unimportant when I remind myself of Him and His will. Then, like Asaph, I am satisfied.

Points to Ponder

1. Do you find yourself under God's steady, disciplining hand? Or are you struggling with anger just below the surface because the Lord does not honor your desires? Neither attitude produces peace. Recognize how God deals with us and our attitudes toward Him. In either case, you need an attitude adjustment.

2. Write down some areas where you currently struggle.

3. What steps must you take to align yourself with God's desires, not yours?

Self-Condemnation

This section is akin to the section entitled *Inner Peace*. However, several nuances appear here that are worthy of notice.

First, people often struggle with self-acceptance or God-acceptance. If we don't experience peace with God, we will not have peace with others. As a pastor, I see this in many people. These folks never feel worthy of God's love, mercy and grace. This attitude handcuffs them, so they never attempt to produce fruit for the Lord (John 15).

The great news is that no one is worthy of God's love, mercy and grace! That's why salvation is so beautiful. We find rest and peace in Him.

Regarding self-condemnation, consider the words and actions of the following three accounts: Pilate's wife, the woman with the unstaunched flow of blood and a leper. What links these three? All struggled in their relationships with God.

- "While he [Pilate] was sitting on the judgment seat, his wife sent to him, saying, 'Have nothing to do with that just Man, for I have suffered many things today in a dream because of Him'" (Matthew 27:19). Pilate vacillated between releasing Jesus and condemning him. The presence of "this just Man" troubled Pilate's wife, and her statement added another layer of uncertainty to Pilate's decision. Neither enjoyed a season of peace.

- "And suddenly, a woman who had a flow of blood for twelve years came from behind and touched the hem of His garment. For she said to herself, 'If only I may touch

His garment, I shall be made well'" (Matthew 9:20-21). She felt unworthy to approach Christ directly. Christ did not let her hide but had her testify about her healing!

- Immediately after the Sermon on the Mount, a leper approached Jesus—something unheard of in the ancient world. "And behold, a leper came and worshiped Him, saying, 'Lord, if You are willing, You can make me clean.' Then Jesus put out His hand and touched him, saying, 'I am willing; be cleansed.' Immediately his leprosy was cleansed" (Matthew 8:2-3). Lepers, outcasts of society, had lives filled with guilt and self-doubt. Only Christ could remove them—and He did.

People lament that they cannot be good enough to please God. They are right! In *Deep Change,* Dr. Steve Smith demonstrates the solution to this dilemma. He shows us, "Before I believed in Jesus, I did not have the power to be good for God. After I believed in Jesus, I did not have the power to be good for God. **But what is different now is the Holy Spirit lives in me.**"[23] We still do not have the power to live a "successful, productive life." We never did, and we never will. But the Spirit can produce in us what we fail to achieve on our own. That's grace!

Let's look at the parable of the tax collector and the Pharisee in Luke 18:9-14. Jesus spoke this parable to show how those who humbly seek God discover justification and its accompanying peace, while the arrogance of the Pharisee only increased the chasm between himself and God. In describing the tax collector, the Lord uses a rare term in verse 13 (Greek: ἱλάσκομαι, *hilaskomai*) to show the tax collector's request for forgiveness or atonement is rooted in the shed blood of a sacrifice (ultimately in

---

23   Dr. Steve Smith, *Key to Deep Change: Experiencing Spiritual Transformation by Facing Unfinished Business* (Amazon, Church Equippers, Inc. 2021, Third Edition) 91. Used by permission.

Christ's shed blood). In contrast, the Pharisee's proud demeanor only accentuates his alienation from God. His proud self-sufficiency led to condemnation, without him even knowing it!

> Also, He spoke this parable to some who trusted in themselves that they were righteous and despised others: "Two men went up to the temple to pray, one a Pharisee and the other a tax collector. The Pharisee stood and prayed thus with himself, 'God, I thank You that I am not like other men — extortioners, unjust, adulterers, or even as this tax collector. I fast twice a week; I give tithes of all that I possess.' And the tax collector, standing afar off, would not so much as raise *his* eyes to heaven but beat his breast, saying, 'God, be merciful [propitious] to me, a sinner!' I tell you, this man went down to his house justified *rather* than the other, for everyone who exalts himself will be humbled, and he who humbles himself will be exalted."

People often feel condemned because they cannot measure up. They are right. We cannot measure up. However, our Lord Jesus Christ does measure up, and He endows us with his perfect righteousness (2 Corinthians 5:21). After we trust Christ alone for salvation, God sees us "in Christ." However, those who are arrogant and self-righteous desperately need the righteousness found in Christ alone.

When we fail, those failures tend to haunt us. I know this is true of me. My bent is to beat myself up over my failures. Growing up, it seemed like everyone reminded me that I was never good enough. Parents, coaches, teachers and even my friends. My response: try harder—only to be told again that my efforts were not good enough.

The old axiom, "Hurting people hurt people," rings true. A phrase made popular on Social Media states, "If you never heal from what hurt you, you'll bleed on people who didn't cut you."[24] This scenario plays out regularly. Therefore, we must understand how to overcome self-condemnation.

I often think of Peter's failure when he denied Christ three times, as predicted in Luke 22:31-34. The Lord allowed Peter to fail while continuing to pray for His disciple!

> And the Lord said, "Simon, Simon! Indeed, Satan has asked for you, that he may sift *you* as wheat. But I have prayed for you, that your faith should not fail; and when you have returned to *Me,* strengthen your brethren." But he said to Him, "Lord, I am ready to go with You, both to prison and to death." Then He said, "I tell you, Peter, the rooster shall not crow this day before you will deny three times that you know Me."

One description of Peter's denial of Christ is found in Luke 22:54-61. Verses 60-61 powerfully demonstrate the aftermath of Peter's failure.

> Immediately, while he was still speaking, the rooster crowed. **And the Lord turned and looked at Peter.** Then Peter remembered the word of the Lord, how He had said to him, "Before the rooster crows, you will deny Me three times" (emphasis mine).

---

24   This quote is attributed to TobyMac. However, Reddit recognizes that the orign of this quote is unknown.

Imagine Peter's sense of utter failure and condemnation. The Lord did not allow Peter to remain in that failed state. The Lord met him on his "surf" (John 21) at the Sea of Galilee. Note some striking incidents from Peter's life as a disciple. First, the miraculous catch of fish (John 21:6) is reminiscent of the miraculous catch described in Luke 5:1-9. At that point, the Lord commissioned Peter to "catch men." This miraculous catch was more than a subtle reminder to Peter of his ministry to catch men, not fish. Second, the term used to describe the "charcoal fire" (Greek, *anthrakia*) is found in only two places in the New Testament. In John 18:18, Peter warmed himself by a fire of coals in the courtyard of the High Priest during Jesus' trial when Peter denied knowing Christ. Then the fish were cooked over a fire of coals (John 21:9). No doubt the aroma of this fire of coals reminded Peter of his failure to identify with Christ on the night of His betrayal. Third, Jesus asked Peter three times, "Do you love me?" Jesus' first two queries used the word *agapaō (Greek,* ἀγαπᾷς, a kind of love that longs for reciprocity but does not demand it). This is the kind of love God has for people. Peter responds to the first two queries, "Lord, You know I love (*phileō)* you" (*Greek, phileō* —the root word for brotherly love). *Phileō* love is love indeed, but not the highest kind of love sought by the Savior. *Philō* is a love of reciprocity. (Perhaps Peter learned a lesson about being too rash in his response and toned back his reply.)

Finally, in John 21:17, to drive home his point, the Lord asks Peter a third question: "Do you love me" (*philō*). Peter was grieved because He said to him a third time, "Do you love Me?" Peter's response, "Lord, You know all things; You know that I love (*philō*). You."

The Lord used this occasion to confront the failure while affirming Peter's future ministry "to feed my lambs and tend my sheep." His failure was not final. Grace prevailed! Hallelujah.

I wonder if Peter's thoughts drifted back to his denial of Christ every time he heard a rooster crow. I know that sights, sounds and even aromas often remind me of my failures.

Many years ago, I received a phone call from a member of our church. As the end of his earthly life drew near, he wanted to talk privately with me about his eternal destiny. We drove to a remote area of his farm. When we began our conversation, a flood of emotion poured from his soul. His concern: would he measure up when he stood before the Lord? He said, "I've been faithful to my wife and loved my children. I've worked hard. Will that be enough?" I asked him if he had trusted Christ as his Savior. He assured me that this occurred over sixty years before. So I looked him in the eye and said, "What you have done in life will never be enough. However, what Christ has done for you is sufficient." We spoke for a long time. This octogenarian sobbed as he allowed the truth of the gospel to soak into his soul. He died shortly after this, satisfied in Christ!

This friend struggled inwardly for years with his insecurity—an insecurity that looked to human merit, not Christ's finished work. I've noted that many of his generation struggled in the same way. As the sand in their hourglass trickles out, they do not have assurance in the finished work of Christ. Consequently, they struggle with self-acceptance and God-acceptance.

Point to Ponder

1. Do you struggle with feelings of inadequacy?

2. Apply these truths to your troubled soul as you wrestle with your self-worth in Christ!

Spiritual Warfare

Spiritual warfare is a vital subject. Some tend to overemphasize the concept and want to see a demon behind every rock, while others feel it is ridiculous since they think that Satan is powerless over believers. However, the Word of God is clear—spiritual warfare is real. Unfortunately, American Christians too often neglect the hint found in 2 Corinthians 2:11. In this text, the Apostle reminds the church to forgive a repentant believer rather than continuing to ostracize him.

> Now, whom you forgive anything, I also *forgive*. For if indeed I have forgiven anything, I have forgiven that one for your sakes in the presence of Christ, lest Satan should take advantage of us, for we **are not ignorant of his devices** (emphasis mine).

All too often, I fear, we are ignorant of Satan's devices. Satan and his minions wormed their way into the Corinthian believers' hearts to produce unforgiving bitterness. As a pastor, I encounter too much of this attitude.

The attacks from the enemy originate from Satan and his directed demonic activity, from malicious and vicious unbelievers, or even from believers, some of whom are well-meaning, while others may become intentionally vicious. Regardless of the direction of attack, spiritual warfare is an unpleasant reality. Therefore, we must be spiritually prepared for these attacks.

- *Direct Attacks from Satan*
- *Attacks from Vicious Unbelievers*
- *Attacks from Believers*
- *Spiritual Preparation*

Direct Attacks from Satan

The Word of God shows Satan and his henchmen directly assaulting believers. Following the repatriation of Israel after the Babylonian captivity, Joshua, the High Priest, found himself targeted by Satan. We also see the Lord's provision for his servant!

> Then he showed me Joshua, the high priest, standing before the Angel of the LORD, and Satan standing at his right hand to oppose him. And the LORD said to Satan, "The LORD rebuke you, Satan! The LORD, who has chosen Jerusalem, rebuke you! *Is* this not a brand plucked from the fire?" —Zechariah 3:1-2.

We also see how the Lord used the assaults of Satan to chastise proud Israel through David, their king.

> Now Satan stood up against Israel and moved David to number Israel. —1 Chronicles 21:1

The other side of this challenge is further explained in 2 Samuel 24:1-21. The text tells us that the Lord "moved David against them (Israel) to say, 'Go, number Israel and Judah.'" Here, we see the intersection of Divine rule and Satan's activity. The Lord used this event to secure the Temple Mount in Jerusalem for the construction of Solomon's temple while concurrently disciplining David and Israel for their pride. The Lord did not tempt David to sin, which is impossible (see James 1:13).

The enemy of our souls uses our fleshly weaknesses against us. He knows which buttons to push. Therefore, we must be aware! Here is an example of Satan's temptation of married couples.

> Do not deprive one another except with consent for a time, that you may give yourselves to fasting and prayer, and come together again so that Satan does not tempt you because of your lack of self-control. —1 Corinthians 7:5

Satan can hinder us in our mission as we seek to serve the Lord as seen in 1 Thessalonians 2:18. "Therefore, we wanted to come to you –even I, Paul, time and again—but Satan hindered us."

Satan relentlessly attacks and opposes Christ-followers. Observe the following passages. In Matthew 13:19, Satan snatches the word away from those who hear the gospel but do not understand it. In Luke 22:21, Satan desired "to sift Peter as wheat." Consider also Acts 5:3 and 2 Corinthians 11:14, 15.

He, likewise, assaults us before God in heaven. Satan is relentless in his quest to destroy believers.

> Then I heard a loud voice saying in heaven, "Now salvation, and strength, and the kingdom of our God, and the power of His Christ have come, for the accuser of our brethren, who accused them before our God **day and night**, has been cast down. So the great dragon was cast out, that serpent of old called the Devil and Satan, who deceives the whole world; he was cast to the earth, and his angels were cast out with him. Then I heard a loud voice saying in heaven, "Now salvation, and strength, and the kingdom of our God, and

the power of His Christ have come, for the accuser of our brethren, who accused them before our God day and night, has been cast down (emphasis mine). –Revelation 12:8-10

The enemy's attacks against God's people are relentless and vitriolic. I believe it was Warren Wiersbe who once said, "When Satan speaks to us about God, he lies. When he speaks to God about us, he tells the truth!"

Points to Ponder

1. Can you identify a season of life when Satan attacked you?

2. What was his focus during the attack?

3. How did you respond?

Attacks from Vicious Unbelievers

Vicious and malicious attacks from unbelievers are often directed toward believers.

Now, about that time, Herod the king stretched out *his* hand to harass some from the church. Then he killed James, the brother of John, with the sword. And because he saw that it pleased the Jews, he proceeded further to seize Peter also. Now, it was *during* the Days of Unleavened Bread. —Acts 12:1-3

Notice how mob dynamics played into the following attack.

> But the multitude of the city was divided: part sided with
> the Jews and part with the apostles. And when a violent at-
> tempt was made by both the Gentiles and Jews, with their
> rulers, to abuse and stone them, they became aware of it
> and fled to Lystra and Derbe, cities of Lycaonia, and to the
> surrounding region. —Acts 14:4-6

The preaching of the gospel threatened the livelihood of the sil-
versmiths in Ephesus. Consequently, these individuals violently
protested against Paul and his companions in Acts 19:23-40.

Note that Satan may have a mailing address. The Lord said the
following when speaking to the church in Pergamos.

> I know your works, and where you dwell, where Satan's
> throne *is*. And you hold fast to My name, and did not deny
> My faith even in the days in which Antipas *was* My faithful
> martyr, who was killed among you, where Satan dwells.

These passages are a small sample of the persecution suffered
by the early believers. All this suffering concords with Christ's
promise of trouble in John 15:20: "If they persecuted me, they
also will persecute you."

Points to Ponder

1. Generally, we do not suffer from violence in the US as
   many believers in other parts of the world suffer, though
   violence is a growing problem. These kinds of attacks
   from vicious unbelievers will undoubtedly increase.

2. How prepared are you to stand in times like these?

Attacks from Believers

Some of the most difficult issues for me to handle come from the hands of fellow believers. I think, "Lord, this isn't fair. We're supposed to be on the same team." In the section below, we see believers attacking others. In the first case, Peter became a tool of Satan to attack the Lord Himself.

> Matthew 16:23 But He turned and said to Peter, "Get behind Me, **Satan**! You are an offense to Me, for you are not mindful of the things of God, but the things of men" (emphasis mine).

> A brother sins against another brother –Matthew 18:15-18

> Now I urge you, brethren, note those who cause divisions and offenses contrary to the doctrine which you learned and avoid them. For those who are such do not serve our Lord Jesus Christ, but their own belly, and by smooth words and flattering speech deceive the hearts of the simple. –Romans 16:17-18

Some attacks we experience come without rancor. We perceive the attack as personal when no intention to do harm exists. However, sometimes people inflict damage on others, often with evil intent. It happens to all of us.

As believers, we must prepare ourselves for all three different levels of attack. We must prepare ourselves for spiritual warfare. We must remember that Satan is the hater of our souls.

When I pastored in one community, we saw many people come to faith in Christ. During a weekly prayer meeting with other pastors, I declared, "There's hell to pay if we want to grow by evangelism." That's a gross overstatement. However, when we penetrate the domain of Satan, he never takes it lying down. In our case, the most significant opposition came from satisfied church members who gave lip service when they said they wanted to see people come to Christ. Opposition rose when "those people" started coming to faith!

Points to Ponder

1. Have you been the recipient of hardship from the hand of another believer?

2. How did you respond?

3. Have you been the perpetrator of hardship toward another believer?

4. How can you mend fences?

Spiritual Preparation

The Lord reminds us in Ephesians 6:10-20 of the necessary preparation for facing spiritual warfare.

Finally, my brethren, be strong in the Lord and in the power of His might. Put on the whole armor of God that you may be able to stand against the wiles of the devil. For we do not wrestle against flesh and blood, but against principalities, against powers, against the rulers of the darkness of this age, against spiritual *hosts* of wickedness in the heavenly *places*. Therefore, take up the whole armor of God, that you may be able to withstand in the evil day, and having done all, to stand. Stand therefore, having girded your waist with truth, having put on the breastplate of righteousness, and having shod your feet with the preparation of the gospel of peace; above all, taking the shield of faith with which you will be able to quench all the fiery darts of the wicked one. And take the helmet of salvation, and the sword of the Spirit, which is the word of God; praying always with all prayer and supplication in the Spirit, being watchful to this end with all perseverance and supplication for all the saints — and for me, that utterance may be given to me, that I may open my mouth boldly to make known the mystery of the gospel, for which I am an ambassador in chains; that in it I may speak boldly, as I ought to speak.

Four things are evident from this passage. First, we need God's power when confronting the enemy and his demons. The text literally reads that we are to stand in his "mighty might"! Second, the Lord urges us to avail ourselves of His protection. We need what He offers. Third, we must bathe this warfare in prayer. Prayer reminds us of our utter dependence on the Lord. Fourth, the further purpose of the prayer is to give boldness in our testifying for Christ.

Here's a further reason to be on guard.

And no wonder! For Satan himself transforms himself into an angel of light. Therefore, *it is* no great thing if his ministers also transform themselves into ministers of righteousness, whose end will be according to their works. —2 Corinthians 11:14-15

Satan desires to camouflage his activities to make them appear righteous. Famous church fights are always based on someone's interpretation of what's "right!"

Here is an illustration of the insidiousness of the work of Satan in the life of a local church.

> The call came from one of our leaders on Monday. He said, "Do you know what's going around? The word on the street is that you fired our worship leader."
>
> All I could say was, "You've got to be kidding."
>
> No one contacted me directly. The church leader who contacted me heard the scuttlebutt from a third party. The gossip mill churned out the garbage at full speed!
>
> I immediately went to the worship leader's home and visited at length. I needed to leave for another appointment. Sensing that the issue was not yet resolved, I returned on Tuesday afternoon. We finally put all the junk behind us. The remarkable thing: Neither of us started the junk! Someone played host to Satan's devices and deviceness.
>
> My friend, the worship leader, made a rather insightful comment, "All of this happened in the past three weeks **while I was gone**" (emphasis mine). He concluded by stating, "You know, Gordon, I was just caught up in the overwhelming negativism that pervades our church." His observation hit the bullseye!

Spiritual warfare is real. Peter warns us, "Be sober, be vigilant; because your adversary the devil walks about like a roaring lion, seeking whom he may devour" (1 Peter 5:8). The enemy of our souls constantly and deliberately attacks believers and lost people to promote his agenda of ungodliness and the destruction of the souls of men and women, boys and girls, and to discourage and divide believers. As in the case of Nehemiah, sometimes the enemies (Sanballat and Tobiah) were visible. On other occasions, the children of Israel themselves threatened God's work. So it is in the churches. Often, the most devastating attacks come from fellow believers who oppose the work of Christ in our midst.

Two good resources for you as you consider the effects of spiritual warfare are *Bondage Breakers* and *Setting Your Church Free,* both by Neil Anderson. He has produced many other resources that you may find helpful in understanding spiritual warfare.

Points to Ponder

1. Can you identify some of the activities of our enemy at work against you—a direct assault of the enemy of our souls, an assault by wicked unbelievers, or an attack by a fellow Christian?

2. Which proved most painful?

3. What were the circumstances?

4. What was the outcome?

Interpersonal Conflict

As we backed the U-Haul truck up to the front door of the parsonage and raised the door to begin unloading our earthly possessions, the church treasurer approached me and said, "I suppose you know this church is ready to split right down the middle." No one on the pulpit committee bothered to mention this reality to us. When I heard this distressing news, my internal reaction was to reach up, close the U-Haul door and drive away. I didn't. We began an amazing journey of reconciliation that impacted the whole church and our family.

What caused this rift? Interpersonal conflict. Every person "enjoys" the fruit of poor relationships and most possess terrible conflict management skills.

Another pastor friend moved to a church mired in a building project. Once again, no one in the church mentioned the deep, jagged rifts that tore at the heart of this congregation. The pastor said, "When we walked into the church auditorium that first Sunday, you could feel the tension and coldness that permeated the church." Once again, preferences and an unwillingness to deal with conflict issues separated church members into camps—"to build" or "not to build." After two tense years, the church chose to build. A sense of harmony returned, but some rifts continued to rumble below the surface for decades.

When we arrived at that same church many years later, no one told us about the disharmony in the choir. Again, it didn't take long to discover that interpersonal conflict, pride and a tug-of-war existed between the former choir director and the newly appointed leader. The former director claimed no desire to lead but made it impossible for the new leader (or any leader) to do so. These poor interpersonal conflict resolution skills continued to plague this body of believers. In this church, the Lord took me to school to teach me how to handle conflict well. I endured lots of practice!

We will spend much time unpacking the issues that beset believers in the church, people at work or play, and families in the home. At this point, I want us to understand that many different conflict issues exist. Note that each conflict has its own particular prescription. Matthew 18:15-18 is not the go-to passage for every conflict issue. If you wish to get into the meat of this discussion, read Chapter 11 to begin unpacking important principles of managing conflict issues between believers.

Conflict with Our Enemies

Everyone has enemies. It is impossible to avoid having enemies. Instead, the key is to learn how to engage our enemies well. Romans 12:17-21 reads:

> Repay no one evil for evil. Have regard for good things in the sight of all men. **If it is possible, as much as depends on you, live peaceably with all men.** Beloved, do not avenge yourselves, but *rather* give place to wrath; for it is written, "Vengeance *is* Mine, I will repay," says the Lord. Therefore, "If your enemy is hungry, feed him; If he is thirsty, give him a drink; For in so doing you will heap coals of fire on his head." Do not be overcome by evil, but overcome evil with good. (emphasis mine)

This wisdom certainly is absent from many relationships today! In our current culture, many prefer an eye for an eye (or two eyes for an eye) and a tooth for a tooth. If we continue to operate this way (and this was prescribed in the Old Testament), we will be a blind, toothless society! In the eyes of mass shooters, someone often wounded them. Rather than dealing with that person, they exact revenge on many.

Think back to the Columbine shooting on April 20, 1999. Dylan Klebold and Eric Harris felt slighted by their classmates and teachers. Rather than dealing proactively with their tormentors, as they viewed them, they plotted murderous revenge and carried it out. We lived in Wyoming at the time, but this shooting occurred near where we grew up. The carnage shocked and saddened us. Oh, how we need to pursue peace!

Remember the quote, "If you never heal from what hurt you, you'll bleed on people who didn't cut you." Our society runs deep with the blood of revenge! These kinds of travesties will continue until we understand how to deal with unresolved conflict.

Each of us can think of instances where we intersect with difficult people. As I scroll through the deep recesses of my memory, I think of many unreasonable and challenging people. In one case, a family acquaintance lived across the street from an unreasonable, irrational person. We will call her Mrs. B.A. T (remember BA [Bad Attitude] Baracus from the A-Team?). The trigger in this case occurred when the city abandoned part of the street between the two homes where the street dead-ended.

Consequently, the property line between the two lots fell in the middle of the road. The city erected a fence showing the properties' line of demarcation in the middle of what was once the road. The problem occurred when the fence restricted access to a portion of the neighbor's property. Thus began a test of the wills. The neighbor sued the city and challenged their survey (a survey reviewed and approved by three registered Professional

Land Surveyors). On one occasion, the unruly neighbor drove through some recently completed rock landscaping to destroy the hard work of our friend's property. Frequent incursions onto the property became a regular occurrence. Finally, the more docile neighbors placed cameras to observe and record the unsavory activities of the challenging neighbor. The police came on more than one occasion when Mrs. T made threats. Everyone in the neighborhood lived on edge when they encountered Mrs. T.

What solutions might have proved effective? The docile neighbors tried many things—gifts of kindness when a loved one passed, kind smiles and encouraging conversation—all to no avail. One thing that might have helped would have been the removal of the fence. However, Mrs. T lived in misery and shared her miserable wealth with the neighborhood.

So, we must do what we can to live peaceably with everyone as much as it depends on us. We cannot control the attitudes or actions of others. The Lord asks us to do our part.

Points to Ponder

1. List some egregious examples of interpersonal conflict you encountered over the years.

2. How did you feel when you were the target of the attack?

3. Can you recall some instances when others were brutalized? How did that make you feel?

4. How did you respond?

PART 2

Causes of Conflict

- ► THE FIRST CAUSE—SATAN'S FALL AND CONTINUED REBELLION AGAINST GOD
- ► THE PRIMARY CAUSES OF CONFLICT
- ► FLASH POINTS CONTRIBUTING TO CONFLICT

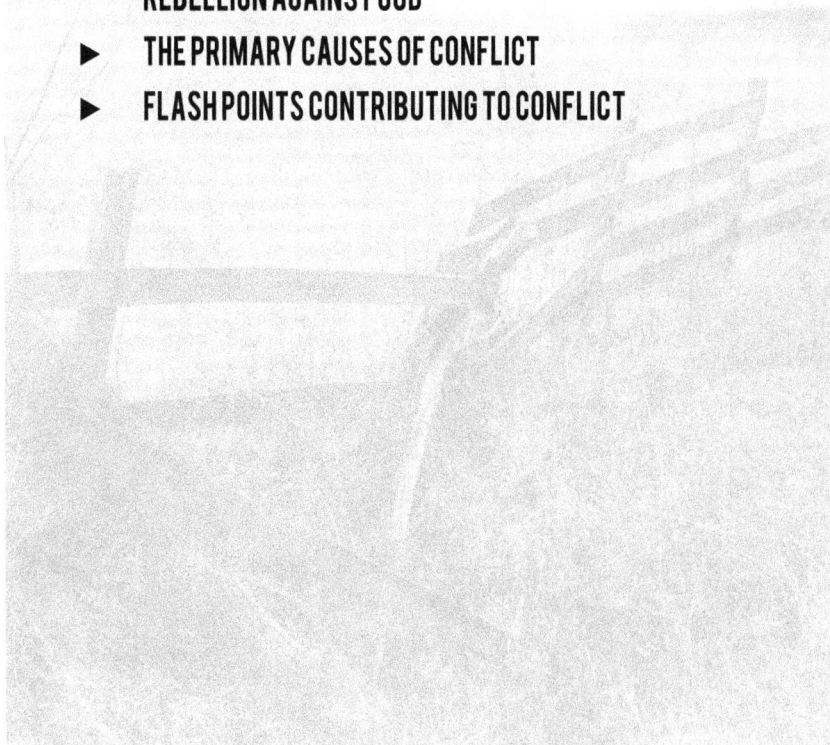

CHAPTER 5

THE FIRST CAUSE—SATAN'S FALL AND CONTINUED REBELLION AGAINST GOD

We are all too aware that conflict swirls about us like great eddies that threaten to suck us into their deep recesses. We feel helpless as people drag us along against our will into the deep cesspools of sin that engulf our society. Unfortunately, we sometimes succumb or strike back in anger, only adding to the mess.

People wonder, "How did we come to this place in life?" Many blame God for our state. However, James 1:13 declares, "Let no one say when he is tempted, 'I am tempted by God,' for God cannot be tempted by evil, nor does He Himself tempt anyone." The Lord allowed for evil without being the author of evil. As we understand the presence of evil from Scripture, it is apparent that the Lord gave free will to His creatures to either follow Him or to rebel against Him. We see this in The First Cause of Evil: Satan's Fall.

Nothing exists without a first cause. In the case of sin and rebellion, that cause is Satan himself. As previously seen, God is not the author of sin. However, He did create beings with free will, including Satan. C. S. Lewis stated the following about omnipotence and free will.

> Finally, it is objected that the ultimate loss of a single soul means the defeat of omnipotence. And so it does. In creating beings with free will, omnipotence from the outset submits to the possibility of such defeat. What you call defeat, I call miracle: for to make things which are not Itself, and thus to become, in a sense, capable of being resisted by its own handiwork, is the most astonishing and unimaginable of all the feats we attribute to the Deity. I willingly believe that the damned are, in one sense, successful, rebels to the end; that the doors of hell are locked on the inside. I do not mean that the ghosts may not wish to come out of hell, in the vague fashion wherein an envious man 'wishes' to be happy: but they certainly do not will even the first preliminary stages of that self-abandonment through which alone the soul can reach any good. They enjoy forever the horrible freedom they have demanded and are therefore self-enslaved: just as the blessed, forever submitting to obedience, become through all eternity more and more free.[25]

In summary, God's greatest act of omnipotence was making creatures who can say "no" to Him! Satan chose to rebel against God. Consequently, he introduced evil into this world. Adam chose to follow Satan's lead, and humanity followed Adam.

The Reality of Satan and Angels. Most people feel frustrated with the current state of affairs, yet we feel helpless to change any outcomes. The problems appear larger than our ability to

---

25   C.S. Lewis, *The Problem of Pain* (Harper Collines Kindle Edition) https://a.co/2LwygQT, 83.

effect meaningful change. To help our understanding of this deep pit in which we find ourselves, we must first understand the ultimate cause of evil. The Scriptures are clear—Satan is the first cause of evil. Angels and Satan exist. Christ, the agent of creation, made them just as He made everything else. Colossians 1:16 states, "For by Him all things were created that are in heaven and that are on earth, visible and invisible, whether thrones or dominions or principalities or powers. All things were created through Him and for Him." Angels have their origin in Christ's creation. At their creation, all angels were good!

The time of the angels' creation is unclear. Job 38:1-7 tells us that the angels were present at the creation of the heavens and earth.

Then the LORD answered Job out of the whirlwind and said:

"Who is this who darkens counsel by words
without knowledge?
Now prepare yourself like a man; I will question you,
and you shall answer Me.
Where were you when I laid the foundations of the earth?
Tell Me, if you have understanding.
Who determined its measurements? Surely you know!
Or who stretched the line upon it?
To what were its foundations fastened?
Or who laid its cornerstone,
When the morning stars sang together,
and all the sons of God shouted for joy?

The phrase "sons of God" refers to angels (see also Job 1:6 and 2:1). The phrase occurs six times in the Old Testament, two other times in Job. So, angels existed at the time of the creation of the earth.

Satan's Fall. A number of evangelical scholars believe Ezekiel 28:12-19 to be a descriptive account of Satan's fall.[26]

Son of man, take up a lamentation for the king of Tyre, and say to him, "Thus says the Lord GOD:

'You were the seal of perfection, full of wisdom and perfect in beauty.
You were in Eden, the garden of God; every precious stone was your covering: the sardius, topaz, and diamond, beryl, onyx, and jasper, sapphire, turquoise, and emerald with gold. The workmanship of your timbrels and pipes as prepared for you on the day you were created.
You were the anointed cherub who covers; I established you. You were on the holy mountain of God. You walked back and forth in the midst of fiery stones. You were perfect in your ways from the day you were created till iniquity was found in you.

By the abundance of your trading, you became filled with violence within, and you sinned. Therefore, I cast you as a profane thing out of the mountain of God, and I destroyed you, oh covering cherub, from the midst of the fiery stones. Your heart was lifted up because of your beauty. You corrupted your wisdom for the sake of your splendor. I cast you to the ground; I laid you before kings that they might gaze at you.

---

26   Scholars include Charles Dyer in *Ezekiel* in *The Bible Knowledge Commentary* (1283), Lewis Sperry Chafer in *Volume II, Systematic Theology* (40-42), Ironside in *Ezekiel* (191-92), and Dickason in *Angels: Elect and Evil* (129-30). On the other hand, Ralph H. Alexander, *Expositor's Bible Commentary, Volume 6*, adopts the view that this passage in Ezekiel applies solely to the king of Tyre, not to Satan (882-884). I believe this description in Ezekiel 28 applies to Satan and best fits the biblical text. This view fits the tenor of other passages, such as Daniel 10:13, where "the prince of Persia withstood me." (This angelic messenger only came to Danel after receiving help from Michael, one of the chief angels. This prince who opposed is obviously an angelic personage. Thus, we see angels, both good and bad, involved in the cosmic struggle for control. Then, in Revelation 2;4, the Lord informs the church at Smyrna that they live in the community where" Satan's throne is." These passages speak to the reality of Satan and his henchmen as they oppose the work of the Lord.

You defiled your sanctuaries by the multitude of your iniquities, by the iniquity of your trading. Therefore, I brought fire from your midst. It devoured you, and I turned you to ashes upon the earth in the sight of all who saw you. **All who knew you among the peoples are astonished at you. You have become a horror and *shall be* no more forever** (emphasis mine).'"

As Dyer explains in *The Bible Knowledge Commentary*, the descriptions in the text go far beyond the King of Tyre.

Ezekiel was not describing an ideal man or a false god in verses 11–26. But his switch from "ruler" to "king" and his allusions to the Garden of Eden do imply that the individual being described was more than human. The best explanation is that Ezekiel was describing Satan, who was the true "king" of Tyre, the one motivating the human "ruler" of Tyre.[27]

Satan's creation included timbrels and pipes (musical instruments) on the day of his creation. His exalted position made his fall all the more untenable. For example, Satan, the anointed cherub who covered, enjoyed an exalted privilege in the mountain of God, walking amid the fiery stones of heaven. Pride emanated from his beauty. His position, beauty and glory were the gift of God. Rebellion was unthinkable.

Some expositors include Isaiah 14:12-17 in the description of Satan's fall.[28] That is certainly possible, but the context of this passage looks more likely to describe the fall of the future king

---

27   Dyer, C. H. (1985). *Ezekiel*. In J. F. Walvoord & R. B. Zuck (Eds.), *The Bible Knowledge Commentary: An Exposition of the Scriptures* (Vol. 1, p. 1283). Victor Books.

28   Dickason in *Angels: Elect and Evil* supports a dual reference to the King of Babylon and Satan (131). Edward J. Young, in *Isaiah*, only attributes this text to apply to the king of Babylon (440-41). He notes that Tertullian, Gregory the Great and other ancients have referred this verse to the fall of Satan,

of Babylon. However, verses 12-14 may be a dual reference to both Babylon and Satan. If this is the case, pride would be the primary impetus for Satan's rebellion. The prideful "I will" reverberates throughout the text.

> How you are fallen from heaven, O Lucifer, son of the morning! How you are cut down to the ground, you who weakened the nations!
> For you have said in your heart:
> "I will ascend into heaven, I will exalt my throne above the stars of God;
> I will also sit on the mount of the congregation on the farthest sides of the north;
> I will ascend above the heights of the clouds,
> I will be like the Most High."
> Yet you shall be brought down to Sheol, to the lowest depths of the Pit.

Satan's rebellion spread to other angels (according to Revelation 12:4) and humanity in Genesis 3. The lying, deception, murder and mayhem spread from the Garden of Eden to every corner of the world inhabited by people.

Satan's Character. The Bible describes Satan's character as a murderer and liar (John 8:44) and as a confirmed and practicing sinner (1 John 3:8). He also promotes a false, deadly lifestyle (Ephesians 2:1-3) while promoting false religious worship (1 Timothy 4:1-3). No wonder we find our world in such a mess!

---

described in Luke 10:18 (441). Young takes strong issue with this view. John A Martin in *Isaiah* in The *Bible Knowledge Commentary*, believes this text refers to Sennacherib, an assertion with some merit, but one that doesn't fit the tenor of the text (Vol 1, 1061).

The Spread of Sin to Humanity. When Satan tempted Eve, he twisted God's words and invited the first couple to "be like God" (Genesis 3:5). Satan passed on to the couple his evil desire to be like God.

When Adam rebelled against God's command, evil permeated Adam and his descendants (see Romans 5:12, where the text tells that the effects of Adam's sin are transmitted to his descendants).[29] The exception is Christ, who was born of the seed of the woman, not the seed of Adam. Hence, Christ is sinless! Little wonder why people behave as they do! Our rebellion results in a lack of personal peace and perpetual conflict with others! In Genesis 3:1-6, the blame game began. Adam blamed Eve, Eve blamed the serpent (Satan), and the serpent "didn't have a leg to stand on!" This also signaled the battle between the "seed of the woman" and the "seed of the serpent." Praise God, the seed of the woman (Christ) prevails!

Satan, though made perfectly in his creation, sought to be equal to God. When this sin overcame him, he became a perpetual enemy of God and people. He came to steal, kill, and destroy, while Christ came to grant people abundant life (John 10:10). Praise the Lord, that in the midst of great turmoil and upheaval, Christ-followers can enjoy peace and purpose!

Points to Ponder

1. How do you view Satan? As one to be placated? As one who can help you attain what you desire? As an enemy?

2. Your perception will impact your life in profound ways.

---

29   Robertson, A. T. (1933). *Word Pictures in the New Testament* (Ro 5:12). Broadman Press.https://ref.ly/logosres/LLS:46.50.2?off=3427194.

CHAPTER 6

THE PRIMARY CAUSES OF CONFLICT

As we observed in the last section, Satan began a process that led to untold suffering and misery. We see this played out on life's stage, act by act, day by day. When we understand the causes of conflict, we become better equipped to handle the enemy's darts hurled at us.

We will examine a litany of issues that plague us personally and in relationships with those in our circle of acquaintances. In this chapter, we will focus on three primary culprits.

- Pride
- The Attitude of the Heart
- Sinful Attitudes that Produce Sinful Actions

Pride

Pride is a prominent theme in biblical literature. The word occurs 48 times in 45 verses (NKJV), most frequently in the Old Testament Wisdom Literature. Pride (Hebrew, גָּאוֹן) has a wide range of meanings. Occasionally, it can take on a positive sense of exaltation or majesty. However, it most frequently maintains a negative connotation, such as pride, haughtiness or arrogance. *The Baker Encyclopedia of the Bible* describes pride in the following ways.

> **Pride**: A reasonable or justifiable self-respect or improper and excessive self-esteem known as conceit or arrogance. The apostle Paul expresses a positive kind of pride when speaking of confidence in Christians (2 Cor 7:4) or of strength in the Lord (2 Cor 12:5, 9). However, it is the latter sinful meaning of pride which most frequently appears in the Bible, both in the OT and the NT.
>
> The 10 Hebrew and 2 Greek words generally used for pride refer to being high or exalted in attitude, the opposite of the virtue of humility . ... One other Greek word refers to a person's being puffed up or inflated with pride or egotism. The idea is that one gives the impression of substance but is really filled only with air (see, e.g., 1 Cor 5:2; 8:1; 13:4; Col 2:18).[30]

Perhaps the most famous passage is Proverbs 16:18: "Pride *goes* before destruction and a haughty spirit before a fall." This statement reverberates off the lips of both Christ-followers and secularists. Listed below are several other Proverbs that speak clearly to the divisiveness and destructiveness of pride (emphases mine).

- Proverbs 11:2: When **pride** comes, then comes shame; But with the humble *wi*sdom.

- Proverbs 13:10: By **pride** comes nothing but strife, But with the well-advised *is* wisdom.

---

30   Elwell, W. A., & Beitzel, B. J. (1988). Pride. In *Baker Encyclopedia of the Bible* (Vol. 2, p. 1752). Grand Rapids, MI: Baker Book House.

- Proverbs 21:24: "A proud *and* haughty *man*— *'Scoffer'* is his name; He acts with arrogant **pride**."
  Scoffers are those who deride others while exalting themselves. This results in shame, hurt, and anger.
- Psalm 10:2: The wicked in *his* **pride** persecutes the poor; Let them be caught in the plots which they have devised.
- Matthew 7:21-23: For from within, out of the heart of men, proceed evil thoughts, adulteries, fornications, murders, thefts, covetousness, wickedness, deceit, lewdness, an evil eye, blasphemy, **pride**, foolishness. "All these evil things come from within and defile a man.

The Lord offers a strong rebuke against pride in 1 John 2:15-16.

> Do not love the world or the things in the world. If anyone loves the world, the love of the Father is not in him. For all that *is* in the world—the lust of the flesh, the lust of the eyes, and the **pride of life**—is not of the Father but is of the world (emphasis mine).

Years ago, I had a conversation with a retired pastor. He met a fellow believer and spoke to him about spiritual things. The man admitted, "I haven't been to church for over thirty years." The pastor asked, "What happened?"

"Thirty-odd years ago, my church purchased a new piano for the auditorium. We had a big kerfuffle about which side of the auditorium to place the piano. The church didn't place it on the side I wanted."

At that point, the pastor asked, "Which side was that?" The man responded, "I don't even remember!"

Pride causes all kinds of division, heartache and pain. Often, it is over foolish things! I have also noted that the fuzzier the issue, the greater the heat and smoke generated!

At a retreat a few years back, two pastors, both alpha males, could be a bit hotheaded. One was a martial arts expert, and the other was an avid outdoorsman who loved hunting and fishing. The two got into a heated discussion about which was better, martial arts or guns. (Remember, the less clarity of the issue, the greater the heat and smoke!). Suddenly, one pastor shouted at the other pastor across the room, "I'll take my 45, and you bring your martial arts. You start at me from the other side of the room, and I will stand here. Come at me! We will see who's left standing when the smoke clears."

The sad part of this encounter is that they were both deadly serious. Pride destroyed their relationship and shook all who witnessed the spectacle!

Points to Ponder

1. How much does your pride influence your life and relationships with others?

2. Have you allowed pride to destroy a relationship? To harm a fellow pilgrim?

3. What steps should you take to mend fences where your pride has broken relationships?

The Attitude of the Heart

I remember hearing the story of a prank pulled on a college student living in a dorm. This fellow was known to sleep deeply. As he slept one afternoon, some friends slipped into his room and spread a little Limburger Cheese on his mustache. His lip twitched a bit, but he did not awaken. Later, when he awoke, he said, "Man, this room stinks!" Seeking relief from the stench, he walked into the hallway, saying loudly, "This hallway stinks!" With that, he went outdoors to seek a break from the odor. Much to his chagrin, life did not improve. There, he shouted, "The whole world stinks!" He did not realize the whole time that the problem was just under his nose!

Our problem is not Limburger Cheese and our olfactory tissue. The problem runs deeper. It lies in our heart, not the physical organ, but what the Bible describes as the center of our being. Reflect on the following passages.

> Brood of vipers! How can you, being evil, speak good things? For out of the abundance of the heart, the mouth speaks. —Matthew 12:34

> Do you not yet understand that whatever enters the mouth goes into the stomach and is eliminated? But those things which proceed out of the mouth come from the heart, and they defile a man. For out of the heart proceed evil thoughts, murders, adulteries, fornications, thefts, false witness, blasphemies. —Matthew 15:18-19

> A good man out of the good treasure of his heart brings forth good, and an evil man out of the evil treasure of his heart brings forth evil. For out of the abundance of the heart, his mouth speaks. —Luke 6:45

Where do wars and fights come from among you? Do they not come from your desires for pleasure that war in your members? You lust and do not have. You murder and covet and cannot obtain. You fight and war. Yet you do not have because you do not ask. You ask and do not receive because you ask amiss, that you may spend it on your pleasures. —James 4:1-3

A cursory review of these passages points to the source of our dysfunction and conflict. When we speak evil, that evil flows from the heart. When we think or do wicked things, covet, wish others ill, or struggle with them, the actions proceed out of the heart. Envy, greed, lust, and covetousness all originate deep within us. It's the heart—the center of our being. Jeremiah 17:9 provides a great summary of this thought. "The heart is deceitful above all things and desperately wicked; who can know it?"

Points to Ponder

1. Can you think of a time when pride caused you to act inappropriately toward another individual? What motivated you? Do you need to mend a fence?

2. When you were wronged by someone else, how did you feel? Respond? What motivated this response? Pride or humility?

3. Did you want to strike back? Get even? Make them pay? Perhaps you should check out your heart!

Sinful Attitudes that Produce Sinful Actions

Closely associated with the issues of the heart are the unfortunate outworkings of "the flesh," those sinful impulses that destroy lives and relationships. The Scriptures contain several "sin lists." I wish to only look at one. Galatians 5:16-26 depicts the ongoing warfare between the "flesh" and the Spirit. The first encouragement, a prescription to this problem of fleshly warfare, is to "walk in the Spirit, and you shall not fulfill the lust of the flesh." We must surrender to the Lord to be victorious over those challenges with which we all struggle. The text lists the following challenges presented by the flesh:

List A

Adultery	Fornication
Uncleanness	Lewdness
Idolatry	Sorcery
Hatred	Contentions
Jealousy	Outbursts of wrath
Selfish ambitions	Dissensions
Heresies	Envy
Murders	Drunkenness
Revelries	And the like (this list is not complete!)

Note how these attitudes and actions begin with the heart. Also, notice the close relationship that these actions share—hatred and contentions, for example—or selfish ambitions and dissensions. One bad choice leads to a closely related bad choice gathering momentum like an avalanche.

In contrast to these destructive attitudes and actions, note the fruit of the Spirit produced in the life of a Christ-follower.

List B

Love   Joy
Peace   Longsuffering (patience)
Kindness   Goodness
Faithfulness   Gentleness
Self-control

In Romans 13:14, the Apostle Paul urges us to "put on the Lord Jesus Christ, and make no provision for the flesh, to *fulfill its lusts.*" The Savior and the Holy Spirit both transform our behavior toward godliness!

How would you prefer people around you to show up? List A or B. How would your friends, families, acquaintances and neighbors like you to show up? Only when we walk under the control of the Holy Spirit can we hope to avoid grievous and destructive behaviors outlined in List A.

Points to Ponder

1. Can you think of instances where these attitudes caused broken relationships and heartache?

2. Can you think of instances where you showed up with List A? What was the outcome?

3. Are there fences you must mend because of your fleshly actions?

CHAPTER 7

FLASHPOINTS THAT CONTRIBUTE TO CONFLICT

In this chapter, I'm listing a plethora of issues that cause conflict between people. This enumeration, though extensive, does not exhaust the challenges that wreak havoc in our relationships. Some problems are simple, some deeply complex. All have the potential to blow up our relationships at work, in the home, or in the church. If you have specific troubling issues, scroll down to the section where you find yourself challenged. However, I believe you will find this entire section intriguing. Also, please think of other areas that may cause trouble for you. Please let me know if you see different areas of conflict that you observe. I would love to add them to this list.

- Lack of Agreement on Mission, Vision and Values
- Interpersonal Relationships
- Language Barriers
- Cultural Differences
- Misunderstandings From Poor Communication
- Judging Actions and Motives Incorrectly
- The Tongue

- **Differences Over Personal Preferences**
- **Competition for Limited Resources**
- **Ownership**
- **Traditionalism**
- **Ineffective Leader or Pastor**
- **Controlling or Micromanaging Board, Leader or Pastor**
- **Rebellious Workers or Church Members**
- **Conflict Between the Pioneers and Homesteaders**
- **Poor Fit Between Leader and Company or Pastor and Church**
- **Bullies**
- **Politics, Masks, Vax and Government-Ordered Shutdowns**
- **Assumptions and Unspoken Expectations**
- **Theological and Philosophical Differences**
- **Difficult People and Difficult Situations**
- **Misunderstanding**
- **Money**
- **Other Flash Points**

Lack of Agreement on Mission, Vision and Values

In 2015, I became the intentional interim pastor at a deeply conflicted church in the southern portion of the Denver Metro area.
We slogged through the muck and mire of that church for six
months. The church lacked agreement on its mission and direction and had a lack of clarity on the values that should bind it together. Consequently, the church was not a safe place to belong.
Attacks came from every imaginable direction, and mostly from
church members pitted against one another. During those six
months, I hammered home the Great Commission. We also developed a vision statement for this South Denver Church:

We want to glorify God by providing a **safe place** where

We love like Jesus loves
Forgive like Jesus forgives
Serve like Jesus serves and
Extend grace the way Jesus extends grace
by
Touching 1500 people per year with the love of Christ
Sharing the gospel with 150 people this year
Asking God for 15 new believers this year,

By adding a new Saturday night service within two years
to reach out to those who cannot attend a
Sunday morning service.

We praise the Lord that by His grace, we saw great progress in moving towards health and vitality. Due to a previously scheduled ministry appointment, I concluded my interim ministry after six months. A second interim entered the picture after my departure. The church continued to make progress. However, the second interim said, "If you want to have a ministry, go for it." As a result of this encouragement, several **competing** ministries began. The outcome was more interpersonal challenges and chaos. Fortunately, when the church called a new pastor, he implemented the above-stated vision. After two years, the church moved on from this initial vision because the church grew into a safe haven for believers.

We often see groups of people struggle when their work, ministry or business does not have a clear mission, a clear vision of their objectives and agreed-upon core values. Consequently, these entities possess no clearly spelled-out desired outcomes. A friend who does many church assessments stated, "Churches that do not have clear mission and vision objectives always struggle." Significant conflict is one of the outcomes of a failure to understand and communicate the mission, vision and values. Judges 21:25 tells us that "In those days, *there was* no king in Israel; everyone did *what was* right in his own eyes." The days of the Judges were anything but cohesive and harmonious!

Normally, when a church, business or startup begins, clearly spelled-out goals, objectives and outcomes guide the ship. However, over time, mission and vision drift creep into the picture, and the view of the future becomes fuzzy and out of focus! Figure 1 shows a diagram of most startups, whether churches or businesses. Excitement builds as everyone shares a common mission, vision and values. Special interest groups form. This process is natural and necessary. In a business, these groups may include marketing, sales, manufacturing, R&D and so forth. In a church group, these special interest groups may be Sunday School classes, Women's Ministry, Men's Ministry, Children's Ministry, Youth, Worship Ministry, and so forth. See Figure 1 to gain an understanding of this phenomenon.

Beginning Well
Unifying Mission, Vision, and Values
Special Interest Groups (SIG)

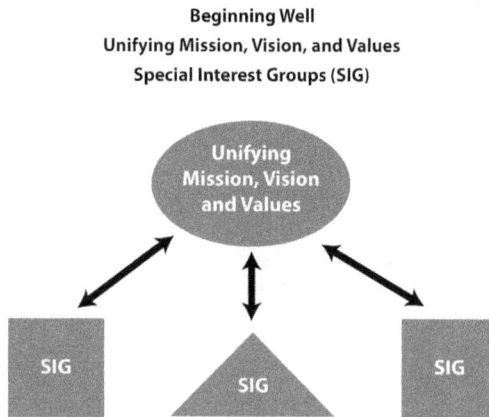

Figure 1

Special Interest Groups are a natural part of the growth and development of any human enterprise. They are needed. Problems arise when the interest groups become self-focused and self-consumed. Without a unifying mission and vision, the groups drift apart. The result is unhealthy competitiveness and territorialism, which is neither productive nor helpful. Figure 2 shows what happens when only special interest groups remain in a church or a company.

Floundering Well
Loss of Unifying Mission, Vision, and Values
And the Remaining Special Interest Groups (SIG)

Without a unifying Mission, Vision, and Values, conflicting interests lead to deepening frustration and conflict.

Figure 2

In the absence of a uniting mission, vision and values, only special interests remain. These groups compete for dwindling resources—people and finances—leading to deepening conflict and frustration. This pattern is common in every arena where people work with others!

In Acts 15:36-40, we see a classic issue of the challenge of a failure to align mission, vision and values. This account involves two of my biblical heroes, Saul, who became known as the Apostle Paul, and Barnabas. Barnabas played a huge role in the development of the Apostle Paul. Barnabas opened ministry doors for Saul and introduced the new "outcast" believer to the Apostles and church in Jerusalem. People in that great city did not trust Saul. This first-century anti-Christian terrorist previously confined many believers in prison and gave his nod to the death of others, including Stephen!

After the gospel exploded in Antioch, Barnabas recruited Saul for ministry in the key Gentile church (Acts 11:15). Later, God used the two of them on a great missionary venture in the Mediterranean and Asia. However, some ripples began to ruffle the surface when Paul rebuked the Apostle Peter and Barnabas for duplicity when Jewish believers arrived at a Gentile feast.

As they prepared for their second missionary journey, a huge dispute arose over whether or not to take John Mark with them. John Mark bailed on the first journey and returned home. Paul did not wish to repeat that failure. He knew the hardship of the venture made loyalty and dependability essential for every team member. Barnabas desired to continue to help John Mark move toward maturity—a process similar to the one he used with Paul. The resulting violent encounter between these two giants of the faith caused them to part ways permanently (so far as we know).

The conflict demonstrates the need for commonality of mission, vision and values. The two agreed on the mission but had different purposes regarding vision and values. The question: "Which is the greater need, developing new missionaries or opening new mission fields?" The more seasoned missionary, Barnabas, held one view. Paul, the gung-ho apostle, maintained the other. Trouble brewed in Acts 15:38-39 when they could not find harmony in all three areas. The chart below illustrates the differences and similarities between Paul and Barnabas and their mission, vision and values.[31]

---

31   *Pastor Unique*, 155. Adapted from my previous work.

	Paul	Barnabas
Mission	Great Commission	Great Commission
Vision	Effective missionary outreach	Developing effective new leaders
Values	Effective ministry now	Effective leaders for the future

Figure 3

As Greek scholar A. T. Robertson enumerated, it's possible that the previous conflict between Peter and Paul in Galatians 2 played into this issue.

A sharp contention (Greek—παροξυσμος [*paroxusmos*]). Our very word paroxysm in English.... This "son of consolation" loses his temper in a dispute over his cousin, and Paul uses sharp words towards his benefactor and friend. It is often so that the little irritations of life give occasion to violent explosions. If the incident in Gal. 2:11-21 had already taken place, there was a sore place already that could be easily rubbed. And if Mark also joined with Peter and Barnabas on that occasion, Paul had fresh ground for irritation about him. But there is no way to settle differences about men, and we can only agree to disagree as Paul and Barnabas did. **So that they parted asunder from one another....**

No one can rightly blame Barnabas for giving his cousin John Mark a second chance nor Paul for fearing to risk him again. One's judgment may go with Paul, but one's heart goes with Barnabas. And Mark made good with Barnabas, with Peter (1 Peter 5:13), and finally with Paul (Col. 4:10; 2 Tim. 4:11).[32]

---

32   Robertson, A. T. (1933). Word Pictures in the New Testament (Ac 15:39). Broadman Press. https://ref.ly/logosres/LLS:46.50.2?off=1988780.

What's the solution? Clarify, communicate, influence, align, and empower those in the church or company to accomplish the clearly stated and agreed mission, vision and values. Do not let little irritations turn into huge gaping sores that ruin relationships!

Birkman International, a company that helps people achieve greater productivity, notes the following about "purpose." In church settings, we would refer to our mission. Regardless of the title, a clear understanding of who we are and our future direction improves relationships.

Your Team's North Star

Like culture, purpose is defined at both the organizational and team levels. Yet many leaders focus on purpose as a uniter of the organization and neglect the importance it plays for individual teams. As Forbes notes, "In a world demanding more agility, establishing a team purpose is foundational to inspiring peak performance."

How does purpose relate to teams? We define it as the reason the team exists, how they contribute to the organization, and their role in how they benefit stakeholders and customers. It is the North Star that does several important things for teams:

- Guides why they do what they do
- Creates a common bond between team members
- Connects the team to the organization and individuals within the team

- When a team does not understand its purpose, cultural dynamics and employee engagement are put at risk. [33]

In your ministry or group, can you identify your North Star? Doing so will help you better fulfill your purpose and avoid unnecessary challenges.

Points to Ponder

1. Can you think of seasons of conflict that arose from a lack of agreement on the mission, vision or values?

2. What were the outcomes of the fray?

3. Did the parties reconcile? Why or why not?

Interpersonal Relationships

Interpersonal relationships are inescapable. We relate to people regularly. Some thrive on these relationships and derive energy from them (extroverts), while others recharge in quiet places (introverts). However, both groups interact with people. Great interpersonal relationships make life enjoyable; however, bad relationships sour life, like eating a green persimmon. We generally do not ask for trouble, but challenging relationships test us to the limits.

---

33   Birkman International, "The Engaged Workplace: How to Create a Winning Team Culture. A guide to building a vibrant workplace culture that keeps teams engaged," Accessed July 22, 2023.

The Apostles Peter, Paul and Barnabas experienced a traumatic situation in Caesarea. I alluded to this in the last section. Here is the account. Some people's actions were contrary to the gospel, and Paul rebuked them soundly! I'm certain tensions were high in the room!

> Now, when Peter had come to Antioch, I withstood him to his face, because he was to be blamed; for before certain men came from James, he would eat with the Gentiles; but when they came, he withdrew and separated himself, fearing those who were of the circumcision. And the rest of the Jews also played the hypocrite with him so that even Barnabas was carried away with their hypocrisy. But when I saw that they were not straightforward about the truth of the gospel, I said to Peter before *them* all, "If you, being a Jew, live in the manner of Gentiles and not as the Jews, why do you compel Gentiles to live as Jews? We *who are* Jews by nature, and not sinners of the Gentiles, knowing that a man is not justified by the works of the law but by faith in Jesus Christ, even we have believed in Christ Jesus, that we might be justified by faith in Christ and not by the works of the law; for by the works of the law no flesh shall be justified. But if, while we seek to be justified by Christ, we ourselves also are found sinners, *is* Christ, therefore, a minister of sin? Certainly not! For if I build again those things which I destroyed, I make myself a transgressor. For I, through the law, died to the law that I might live to God. I have been crucified with Christ; it is no longer I who live, but Christ lives in me; and the *life* which I now live in the flesh I live by faith in the Son of God, who loved me and gave Himself for me. I do not set aside the grace of God; for if righteousness *comes* through the law, then Christ died in vain." —Galatians 2:11-21

This incident was a serious breach of the gospel when they "became Jews" around the Jews, though they behaved as Gentiles when the other Jews were not present. Conflict? Yes! Necessary? Yes! Doctrinal and ethical purity necessitated this conflict. Some of the great declarations concerning the gospel rose from this incident. The great declaration of our standing in grace in Galatians 2:20 flowed out of this controversy!

In Revelation 2:20, Jesus Himself addresses a breach of conduct in the church at Thyatira. He leveled His displeasure with the church for allowing Jezebel to "teach and seduce My servants to commit sexual immorality and eat things sacrificed to idols." Interpersonal conflict? Yes, at the highest level!

Matthew 18:15-18 is another passage that deals with interpersonal conflict. We will address this issue along with many other challenges in Part 4.

Points to Ponder

1. Can you think of a time when you tried to do the right thing, and it turned out badly?

2. Was that painful?

3. How did you attempt to mend fences?

Language Barriers

Language barriers can create great problems for people. It all started at the Tower of Babel, as described in Genesis 11. I will never forget my first foray into the Former Soviet Union. The confusion of language moved front and center. When the plane landed at Borispol airport in Kyiv, I heard unintelligible language. Only after great difficulty, I learned to speak a little Russian. When I traveled to Western Ukraine, I needed to begin to learn Ukrainian. It is far different than Russian. I commented, "When God confused the languages at Babel, He did a great job!"

The language barrier problem showed up in Acts 6 when there was an issue in the fledgling church between Hebraic-speaking Jews and Greek-speaking Jews. Divisions already existed in Israel between those from Jerusalem and Galilee. It was said, "If anyone wishes to be rich, let him go north [Galilee]; if he wants to be wise, let him come south [Jerusalem]."[34] Language and natural divisions between these two groups became evident during the church's explosive growth in the first century.

> Now, in those days, when *the number of* the disciples was multiplying, there arose a complaint against the Hebrews by the Hellenists because their widows were neglected in the daily distribution. Then the twelve summoned the multitude of the disciples and said, "It is not desirable that we should leave the word of God and serve tables. "Therefore, brethren, seek out from among you seven men of *good* reputation, full of the Holy Spirit and wisdom, whom we may appoint over this business; but we will give ourselves continually to prayer and to the ministry of the word." And the saying pleased the whole multitude. And they chose

---

34   Alfred Eidersheim, *Sketches of Jewish Social Life in the Days of Christ* Chapter 3. Sketches of Jewish Social Life in the Days of Christ (Illustrated) (Christian Cultural Treasury) https://a.co/2VwpF2P

Stephen, a man full of faith and the Holy Spirit, and Philip, Prochorus, Nicanor, Timon, Parmenas, and Nicolas, a proselyte from Antioch, whom they set before the apostles; and when they had prayed, they laid hands on them. Then the word of God spread, and the number of the disciples multiplied greatly in Jerusalem, and a great many of the priests were obedient to the faith. —Acts 6:1-7

To overcome these language challenges, we must be proactive like the apostles and the early church. The apostles took immediate action and charged the selection of the Seven to the church membership. The church body made wise choices. All those chosen bore Greek names. The Hellenists knew their needs would be met. The apostles placed their stamp of approval on the Seven.

The result of this investiture: The number of disciples multiplied. The mission moved forward!

In our country, we face these same kinds of issues. Multiple languages grace our land, but these cultural and linguistic differences make people uncomfortable and can create conflicts. I experienced these same attitudes and reactions toward me when I traveled abroad. I saw the looks and felt the scorn of some of the locals. In a church on the West Coast, people in the 18,000-member local school district lived in homes where families represented 100 different language groups. This church demonstrated a great missionary zeal abroad but ignored the missionary opportunities that lay just outside their front door. We must be proactive in dealing with these differences in Christian love. As we do, the mission will advance!

Points to Ponder

1. How do you react when you hear a language you can't understand?

2. Do you become very "American" and take offense?

3. Do you reach out with hospitality?

Cultural Differences

Cultural barriers often link closely with language barriers. People who speak a language that differs from ours usually observe different customs than we do. These customs may make us uncomfortable or angry! When I was a pastor in Holyoke, Colorado, Vida Abundante, a Spanish-speaking ministry, became a part of our congregation. Most of these wonderful folks came from Mexico. Here is an example of a cultural difference that caused problems between the two groups. In Mexico, people never flush toilet paper down the toilet. They always throw it in the trash. That is the custom because most sanitary sewer systems in Mexico cannot handle toilet paper. I found the same practice in Ukraine for the same reason.

This practice became a problem for our Anglo members. Why? Vida met on Sunday evenings. Our next big activity occurred on Wednesday evening. By Wednesday evening, the smell in the bathrooms became unsavory! Rather than let this issue become a major problem, I spoke with Pastor Ismael and explained the situation. I suggested that Vida Abundante attendees clean out the trash cans on Sunday evening at the end of their services.

That way, we preserved both the Hispanic culture and the olfactory tissue of our Wednesday night crowd. Problem solved without bloodshed!

Points to Ponder

1. Describe a time when a cultural difference challenged you.

2. How did you respond?

3. How could you respond in a better fashion?

Misunderstanding from Poor Communication

Conflicts arising from misunderstandings are among the most common challenges that impact interpersonal relationships. These difficulties arise from something that is said or things we fail to communicate. For example, I verbally process my thoughts and intentions. Consequently, my wife hears multiple options. She assumes that I chose one of those options. She's right! Unfortunately, I don't generally clearly present my final choice. She hears option number four or five when I land on option eight. Two of my close associates operate just like me. The results are the same. Their wives also get upset because all three of us "change our minds." It's not that we change our minds. It's that we process our thoughts without making our final choices clear.

Here is another more serious issue I faced as a pastor. Our church body built a brand new facility in Holyoke, Colorado. Part of our plan was to create a spacious kitchen. We included lots of cupboards—around 70. One of our ladies placed labels on certain cupboards for specific uses. For instance, she labeled three cupboards "Communion." We kept all the serving utensils we used for the Lord's Supper in these spaces. She labeled another "AWANA" and another "Funeral Dinners," and so forth. She put "Vida Abundante" on three cupboards.

I knew something was wrong when I entered the church building one Sunday evening. The large group of ladies from Vida was preparing for a Sunday evening fiesta. This group loves to eat, and I often had the privilege of joining the party! When I entered the kitchen that Sunday, I could sense the tension. They said, "We have this huge kitchen, and we only get three cupboards." Part of the problem is that this group often feels like second-class citizens because American society considers them outsiders and interlopers. Unfortunately, this attitude prevails even in Christian churches.

I quickly found the lady who labeled the cupboards and explained the situation. She was horrified at the miscommunication and immediately went to meet with the ladies from Vida Abundante to explain the labeling system. She said, "The kitchen is for all of us to use. The cupboards identified as for Vida Abundante are for your use only. Other cupboards with labels are for specific uses for specific groups. However, the rest of the kitchen is free to be used by all."

Our "labeler" had the best intentions, but her desires became completely misunderstood. What was obvious to her did not compute with a significant part of our church body. As a result, the potential for damaged relationships existed. Her quick action and explanation averted a relational disaster.

Points to Ponder

1. Can you think of a time when a coworker, friend or family member misunderstood you?

2. What could you have done differently to prevent the difficulty?

3. What did you learn from your experience? How can you use this knowledge in the future?

Judging Actions and Motives Incorrectly

It is so easy to misunderstand someone's motives and actions. Many factors can contribute to this: jealousy or envy, insecurity, or a history of conflict with an individual, to name a few. Often, the stakes are low, but when we misjudge, we open the possibility of damaging our relationships, creating mistrust in our workplace, breaking friendships or worse.

In Joshua 22:10-34, we find an example of poor communication and incorrectly judging motives. This event occurred after Israel's conquest of the Promised Land. Two-and-one-half tribes were free to return to the east side of Jordan to take up their residence assigned to them through Moses. I've included the extended text below. This portion of Scripture shows the misunderstanding and the wise steps employed to settle the resulting conflict.

> And when they came to the region of the Jordan, which *is* in the land of Canaan, the children of Reuben, the children of Gad, and half the tribe of Manasseh built an altar

there by the Jordan — a great, impressive altar. Now the children of Israel heard *someone* say, "Behold, the children of Reuben, the children of Gad, and half the tribe of Manasseh have built an altar on the frontier of the land of Canaan, in the region of the Jordan — on the children of Israel's side." And when the children of Israel heard *of it*, the whole congregation of the children of Israel gathered together at Shiloh to go to war against them. Then the children of Israel sent Phinehas, the son of Eleazar, the priest to the children of Reuben, to the children of Gad, and to half the tribe of Manasseh, into the land of Gilead, and with him ten rulers, one ruler each from the chief house of every tribe of Israel; and each one *was* the head of the house of his father among the divisions of Israel. Then they came to the children of Reuben, to the children of Gad, and to half the tribe of Manasseh, to the land of Gilead, and they spoke with them, saying, "Thus says the whole congregation of the LORD: 'What treachery *is* this that you have committed against the God of Israel, to turn away this day from following the LORD, in that you have built for yourselves an altar, that you might rebel this day against the LORD? *Is* the iniquity of Peor not enough for us, from which we are not cleansed until this day, although there was a plague in the congregation of the LORD, but that you must turn away this day from following the LORD? And it shall be if you rebel today against the LORD, that tomorrow He will be angry with the whole congregation of Israel. Nevertheless, if the land of your possession *is* unclean, *then* cross over to the land of the possession of the LORD, where the LORD's tabernacle stands, and take possession among us; but do not rebel against the LORD, nor rebel against us, by building yourselves an altar besides the altar of the LORD our God. Did not Achan, the son of

Zerah, commit a trespass in the accursed thing, and wrath fell on all the congregation of Israel? And that man did not perish alone in his iniquity.' "

Then the children of Reuben, the children of Gad, and half the tribe of Manasseh answered and said to the heads of the divisions of Israel: "The LORD God of gods, the LORD God of gods, He knows, and let Israel itself know — if *it is* in rebellion, or if in treachery against the LORD, do not save us this day. If we have built ourselves an altar to turn from following the LORD, or if to offer on it burnt offerings or grain offerings, or if to offer peace offerings on it, let the LORD Himself require *an account*. But in fact, we have done it for fear, for a reason, saying, 'In time to come, your descendants may speak to our descendants, saying, "What have you to do with the LORD God of Israel? For the LORD has made the Jordan a border between you and us, *you* children of Reuben and children of Gad. You have no part in the LORD." So your descendants would make our descendants cease fearing the LORD.' Therefore we said, 'Let us now prepare to build ourselves an altar, not for burnt offering nor for sacrifice, but *that* it *may be* a witness between you and us and our generations after us, that we may perform the service of the LORD before Him with our burnt offerings, with our sacrifices, and with our peace offerings; that your descendants may not say to our descendants in time to come, "You have no part in the LORD." ' Therefore we said that it will be, when they say *this* to us or to our generations in time to come, that we may say, 'Here is the replica of the altar of the LORD which our fathers made, though not for burnt offerings nor for sacrifices; but it *is* a witness between you and us.' Far be it from us that we should rebel against the LORD, and turn from following the LORD this day, to build an altar for burnt offerings, for grain offerings, or for sacrifices, besides the altar of the LORD our God which *is* before His tabernacle."

Now, when Phinehas, the priest, and the rulers of the congregation, the heads of the divisions of Israel who *were* with him, heard the words that the children of Reuben, the children of Gad, and the children of Manasseh spoke, it pleased them. Then Phinehas, the son of Eleazar, the priest, said to the children of Reuben, the children of Gad, and the children of Manasseh, "This day we perceive that the LORD *is* among us because you have not committed this treachery against the LORD. Now you have delivered the children of Israel out of the hand of the LORD." And Phinehas, the son of Eleazar, the priest, and the rulers, returned from the children of Reuben and the children of Gad, from the land of Gilead to the land of Canaan, to the children of Israel, and brought back word to them. So the thing pleased the children of Israel, and the children of Israel blessed God; they spoke no more of going against them in battle, to destroy the land where the children of Reuben and Gad dwelt. The children of Reuben and the children of Gad called the altar, *Witness*, "For *it is* a witness between us that the LORD *is* God."

Notice the following:

1. The difficulty began with a rumor based on partial truth. "Our Eastern brothers built an altar," which was true, but not the whole truth.

2. The issue was significant. Israel experienced severe judgment at the hand of the Lord for their idolatrous

and lustful practices at Baal Peor. The nine-and-one-half tribes did not desire to experience a repeat of God's wrath.

3. The nine-and-one-half tribes prepared to settle the issue by force of arms, if necessary.

4. They investigated before acting.

5. Once they cleared up the misunderstanding, everyone returned to their inheritance.

Here is a summary of the process:

1. The report
2. The response to investigate
3. The research
4. The resolution
5. The return to normalcy

This interaction provides a good pattern to follow when dealing with a misunderstanding. Understand the significance of the issue. Be prepared to handle the problem. Investigate. Respond appropriately.

Too often, people are afraid to act in this manner. They prefer to hide out in their insecurity. Act appropriately. Your emotional health and the health of your relationships are too important to ignore.

Points to Ponder

1. Have you experienced a misunderstanding?

2. How did you approach the issue?

3. What was the result? Good? Bad? Why?

4. What did you learn from your experience?

The Tongue

The tongue is a small part of the body, but it causes great damage. Broken relationships, severed friendships, dysfunctional families, heartache and any number of ills start with the flapper between the roof of our mouth and our jaw. On occasion, words meant to heal produce pain and division. Unfortunately, there are times when we intend to inflict pain. It's happened to me. I imagine it's happened to you. James provides a graphic description of the tongue for us.

> For we all stumble in many things. If anyone does not stumble in word, he *is* a perfect man, able also to bridle the whole body. Indeed, we put bits in horses' mouths that they may obey us, and we turn their whole body. Look also at ships: although they are so large and are driven by fierce winds, they are turned by a very small rudder wherever the pilot desires. Even so, the tongue is a little member and boasts great things. See how great a forest a little fire kindles! And the tongue *is* a fire, a world of iniquity. The tongue is so set among our members that it defiles the whole body and sets on fire the course of nature, and it is set on fire by hell. For every kind of beast and bird, of reptile and creature of the sea, is tamed and has been tamed by mankind [humanity]. But no man can tame the tongue. *It is* an unruly evil, full of deadly poison. With it, we bless our God and Father, and with it, we curse men who have

been made in the similitude of God. Out of the same mouth proceed blessing and cursing. My brethren, these things ought not to be so. Does a spring send forth fresh *water* and bitter from the same opening? —James 3:2-10

Other passages speak to the destructiveness of the tongue. "There is one who speaks like the piercings of a sword, but the tongue of the wise *promotes* health" (Proverbs 12:18). Matthew 12:34 and Matthew 15:18 also speak to the destructiveness of the tongue, but the exposition in James tops the list! The tongue boasts (usually a prescription for trouble), kindles a forest fire (a metaphor for its destructive ability), defiles our whole body and is set on fire by hell.

This text makes clear that no one can tame the tongue. Is there any hope for us? The point: only God can tame the tongue!

I read a grievous account about a woman who took her own life. The suicide note simply read, "They said ..." The lies circulated about her caused such pain that she could not even bear to recount them before ending her life.

The tongue is a deadly fire. The best thing we can do is surrender our tongues and their masters, our hearts, to the Lord!

"O, Lord, protect us from damaging others with our words!"

Points to Ponder

1. Have you used words to inflict pain unintentionally or intentionally on another?

2. Can you think of some situations that raged out of hand because of careless words or words designed to hurt? What was the outcome?

3. How did you respond? Did you stand idly by and watch, or did you enter the fray to help stop the forest fire? Too often, we are bystanders.

4. Describe in your own words the pain that resulted from this.

5. In each case, do you have fences you need to mend?

Differences Over Personal Preferences

We see this play out regularly in life. Someone purchases a new vehicle. Suddenly, this individual becomes the expert on cars and the car you should drive. I saw this as a teenager. In those days, the quarrels were over Chevys and Fords. Classmates even fought over which brand was better. Why? Because we want people to think and be like us. We are most comfortable when people feel like we do. How boring life would be if we succumbed to this thinking.

The same conflicts play out at work, in families and at home. Parents want their kids to complete their unfulfilled dreams. A football star wants his child to be a football star. However, the child may love music or some other activity and have no interest in football.

In the workplace, people magnify their way of completing a job. It may be a good way, but there may be better ways. Nevertheless, we say, "Do your job like I do mine."

In churches, for example, people with the gift of giving may look down on those less free with their finances. Others desire that everyone be involved in their pet ministry, such as AWANA or music.

I am so thankful that the Lord made us all unique! Who would want to attend a church where everyone was a preacher or work in an office where everyone was great at IT? No, we need variety. It's okay to drive a Ford, a Toyota, a Chevy or a Dodge Ram. It's okay to use a PC instead of a Mac. People can choose to homeschool, or send their children to a private school or a public school.

The same is true about whether or not to eat meat, be a vegetarian, or be vegan. The Lord said we can eat what we want as long as we return thanks for it (1 Timothy 4:4).

All of these choices fall into the "gray areas"—areas where the Bible is silent on our choices (see Chapter 3 for a more robust discussion on gray areas). Romans 14-15 and 1 Corinthians 8-10 unpack how we should live "in the gray." It is okay to hold different values as long as our behaviors are not sinful.

> So let no one judge you in food or in drink, or regarding a festival or a new moon or sabbaths, which are a shadow of things to come, but the substance is of Christ.
> —Colossians 2:16-17

Points to Ponder

1. How inflexible are you in the gray areas?

2. Have your preferences created trouble for others? Trouble for you?

3. Where do you need to learn to flex?

Competition for Limited Resources

We already mentioned Abram and Lot (Genesis 13:5-9) as they vied for pasture for their abundant, growing herds and flocks. Abram let Lot choose his real estate. Lot chose poorly, not because of the ground, but because of his new neighbors. Nevertheless, the two men felt the squeeze on their herds.

Workers become unsettled when businesses experience a downturn, fearing the potential of a pink slip. When churches experience lean times, fewer people and financial resources generally stretch ministries to the breaking point. A church I pastored in Wyoming existed in an area rich in uranium. When the Cold War ended, so did the need for uranium. The mines closed. The church body had to reduce every line item in the budget, a process wracked with pain. Indeed, there was competition for shrinking resources.

Even hard times in the home can generate strife. As a young child, our family-run produce company nearly went bankrupt. Christmas was lean that year. My dad left the company and worked whatever jobs he could find. Mom worked in the Sugar Factory lab to help keep us afloat. We all tightened our belts.

Fortunately, my brothers and I managed well. But it was tough to see how our friends fared. They were excited to show their Christmas take! We had little to show in comparison. But we were thankful for the gifts we did receive.

When lean times come, we must recognize that what we enjoyed will no longer be! The Scriptures urge us to seek other people's welfare above our own (Philippians 2:4). This attitude will make leanness easier to bear.

Points to Ponder

1. Have you gone through lean times?

2. What was most difficult?

3. How did you help others?

4. What did you learn through those challenges?

Ownership

When we use the term "Ownership," people can be confused, for they equate ownership with possessing a car, a property or some other tangible item. Ownership can be a good thing or a problem, depending on the context.

Here is an example of good "ownership." Years ago, when I arrived at my second ministry appointment in Southeast Colorado, the church property needed attention. My first thought was,

"Why does the Lord always send us to places that need repair?" The church building was Pepto Bismol Pink, or, as I said, "Pepto Abismal Pink." Apparently, when the Fort Lyon Veterans Administration hospital, situated outside of town, painted much of its extensive campus, they used pink paint. The paint contractor ordered a huge surplus of paint, so the church bought the paint at a discount. The church building, as well as a fair number of residences, became pink. The church was known as "The Pink Church"—not exactly a flattering moniker.

On our first October in Las Animas, we determined to paint the exterior of the building. We gathered on a Saturday and nearly painted the entire exterior, from Pepto Bismol Pink to an adobe sandstone color, a color that fits the region's southwestern theme.

One of our ladies said, "This is no longer the church building. This is my church building, and that wall is my wall because I painted it!" Because of her work on the building, she became much more closely aligned with the church and its purposes. She now "owned" the ministry!

On the other hand, people in churches, businesses, schools, civic organizations and the like become the "owners." That is, they own and run everything and everyone. Any project or undertaking requires the nod of their approval. This behavior is "ownership" in the worst sense of the word.

A pastoral colleague from Iowa attended one of our Advanced Pastoral Training Network sessions high in the mountains of Colorado. He came because he felt stuck and didn't know how to move the ministry forward. A few months after the training, he called me. He said, "I finally know the identity of the church patriarch. Whenever I propose a new direction, we discuss the proposal among the members. Finally, when the time comes to make a decision, everyone looks at this man. If he nods 'yes,' the motion carries. If he folds his arms, leans back in his chair and curls his lip, the answer is 'no.'" It only took eight years for the pastor to discover the church boss. This boss controlled every ministry outcome, stifling innovation and creating a culture of fear and dependence. In a sense, he behaved as a silent bully. This is a clear example of the negative impact of 'bad ownership.'

Every entity has bosses. Some float to the surface like cream, and others bob around like curds. We enjoy blessings when surrounded by cream but agony when dealing with controlling, negatively biased patriarchs or matriarchs. We might call some of these unsavory characters "bullies."

Here's a biblical example of a bad church boss.

> I wrote to the church, but Diotrephes, who loves to have the preeminence among them, does not receive us. Therefore, if I come, I will call to mind his deeds, which he does, prating against us with malicious words. And not content with that, he himself does not receive the brethren, and forbids those who wish to, putting *them* out of the church.
> —3 John 9-10

This example illustrates the destructive power of a leader who seeks personal preeminence and control rather than serving the needs of his constituents. May their tribe fail to reproduce!

Points to Ponder

1. Can you think of examples of "good ownership?" What kind of fruit do you enjoy when working with these individuals?

2. Can you list an example or two of those who exhibited "bad ownership?" What challenges did you face when in the company of these folks?

3. A tough question: Do you display "good ownership" tendencies or "bad?" If your answer is "bad," what must you do to change your approach to working with others?

Traditionalism

Another sticking point that can derail forward progress is traditionalism. Someone defined traditions as "the living faith of those now dead" and traditionalism as "the dead faith of those now living."

Traditionalists tend to object to every proposed change. Their refrains are, "We've never done it that way before" or "We've always done it this way." Anyone who tries to introduce new thoughts or a new way of approaching a difficult task, or anyone whose job is to bring a turnaround to a declining workplace or church, will face the conflict engendered by traditionalism.

I shared these quotes in a church service that experienced a plateau for over twenty years. We saw changes and an uptick in attendance and conversion growth almost immediately. We also shared the challenges that originate with traditionalists.

After the service, one of the matriarchs sought me out with her "traditional" sneer and pointedly stated, "I'm a traditionalist!" There was never a question about this woman's position. She resisted every initiative we proposed. Her attitude also reflected her desire for control (see Diotrephes in 3 John 9!).

Nevertheless, we continued to move forward regardless of her opposition. The sad part of her opposition was that she quietly resisted our efforts while working behind the scenes to sabotage the work of the ministry through others. Others influenced by her negativism began to mimic her persona.

Many companies need change. Flashpoints occur when the rank-and-file desire to keep the status quo the status quo. When companies and churches are stuck, they must change. Henry Ford famously stated, "When you do what you always done, you get what you always got."[35] Good change is always needed, especially in our rapidly changing world. Traditionalists gag when trying to do things differently and desire to choke the life out of any new initiative. It would be best if you did not let them hinder your progress.

Most of us enjoy early adopters. Those in leadership face challenges with late adopters or laggards (never adopters). In leadership, we must focus on those who wish to move forward and not pay so much attention to the squeaky wheels—the traditionalists, though we must still minister to them in love.

---

35   Henry Ford, https://hiddengemprofiles.com/2021/11/
if-you-always-do-what-youve-always-done-youll-always-get-what-youve-always-got-henry-ford/

Points to Ponder

1. How do you respond to change? Early adopter? Late Adopter? Never Adopter?

2. How does your attitude help or hinder your work or ministry? Self-awareness is key to developing and maintaining great relationships with others.

3. What attitude adjustments do you need to implement?

Ineffective Leader or Pastor

Many stuck ministries and businesses become stymied because of ineffective leadership. Perhaps it's the Peter Principle—people get promoted until they reach the level of their incompetence, at which point they no longer get promoted.[36] This phenomenon occurs at work and in the church.

Sometimes, it's a poor fit between the leader and those under him. Too often, rather than address the leadership problem, those with the power to act let the damaging situation continue. Those impacted by the incompetent leader change jobs or churches out of sheer frustration. Seldom do people speak out about an untenable situation. The good news is that we have the freedom to change our jobs or our churches. However, it is sad if we love a church body or enjoy our work and leave because an inept leader steps into leadership. We feel forced out by our unhealthy circumstances.

---

36   https://search.brave.com/search?q=the+peter+principle&source=desktop

I have the privilege of working with multiple churches and multiple pastors. I see the fruit of ineptitude all too often. One church called a pastor I thought would not be a good fit. The church called him despite my warning and, after eighteen months, let him go. He turned out to be arrogant, uncoachable and unaccountable and demonstrated narcissistic tendencies— a growing trend in the leadership world. This is true in the workplace, church and even at home. Consider God's attitude in the following proverb.

> These six *things* the Lord hates,
> Yes, seven *are* an abomination to Him:
> **A proud look, A lying tongue,**
> Hands that shed innocent blood,
> A heart that devises wicked plans,
> Feet that are swift in running to evil,
> A **false witness *who* speaks lies,**
> And **one who sows** discord among brethren.
> —Proverbs 6:6-19 (emphasis mine)

Note how this passage reflects quite a number of issues we examined. Pride does go before a fall!

Points to Ponder

1. I know we all have bad days, but are you working in your "sweet spot?" That is, do you enjoy your work and co-workers?

2. Do you recognize your sweet spot?

3. Describe your work under less-than-desirable conditions. What caused the discomfort? How did you respond?

Controlling or Micromanaging Board, Leader or Pastor

The young pastor was distraught. He did not know which way to turn. After two and a half years of ministry, he felt stuck, unable to move in any direction. He had some good skills but tended to be shy and retiring. The church he pastored experienced continued decline. Three controlling elders compounded the issue. Our team at Advanced Pastoral Network (formerly Turnaround Pastor, Inc.) provided him with assessment, training and coaching through one of our Advanced Pastor Training workshops. We also coached him for a season. Here is one of the exchanges between the pastor and me.

> "Gordon, I just wanted to fill you in before our meeting tonight. The elders have continued their hostility toward me. They met while I was away serving at our youth camp, and then when I got back, they met with me to tell me that I'm being too arrogant and authoritative [my note: The pastor is as mild-mannered as they come. He threatened their control of the church]. They do not see any value in continuing to work on their mission and vision. I spoke with the other members of the team, and they would like to continue. So, there is still tension."

Later, I (Gordon) met with the team, including the elders, on a Wednesday night via Zoom. One elder informed the pastor that he was not coming to the meeting. He was going to travel across the state to do some shopping (He did show up after his bluff). At the end of the meeting, I polled the 13 team members. One of the ladies said, "I've been coming to this church for two years, and I don't have any idea where we are going. I would like to know!" The others agreed, but the elders did not.[37]

We understand that being a pastor requires pastoral leadership and harmony with the deacons and elders of the church. However, no amount of effort served to help relax the grip of the elders. The elders controlled the church and wanted absolute control of the pastor. They viewed the pastor as mere chattel, appointed to serve at the beck and call of their board. He existed to play "Pastor, fetch."[38] Ultimately, the pastor left the church and pastoral ministry for a season. The church continued in a free fall.

On the opposite end of the spectrum, another pastor and his wife micro-managed every ministry in a different church. This behavior proved just as destructive as a micro-managing board. Neither is healthy. There is no limit to what a church can accomplish when a pastor leads, and the church lay leaders and the church body follow.

These real-life examples point to the problem of control and micromanagement. Unfortunately, ambition to control or desire to "protect" people from error or poor leadership often blinds leaders and boards, whether corporate or church. The desire to guard or micromanage hampers what could be a successful venture.

---

37 Personal Correspondence with Pastor D (name withheld), May 2019. This letter came after several months of wrangling with the controlling leadership. The pastor resigned in September 2019.

38 Jeff Patton, If It Could Happen Here (Nashville, Abingdon, 2002), 42. Patton introduced this phrase, which so aptly describes how many pastors are treated as errand boys! Rather, the leaders are to equip the saints to do the work of the ministry (Ephesians 4:12).

I've worked in many different roles, from being a warehouse employee, a team leader, a pastor-servant-leader and working on boards of directors. Most recently, I thoroughly enjoy working with multiple churches and pastors. I struggle with people who wish to micro-manage me or others. That is a great way to stifle progress and snuff out initiative and keep a church, a firm or a gifted leader from accomplishing the goals and mission of the organization. Part of that struggle comes from my desire for freedom and part from my desire to contribute to the effort in my appointed role using my gifts and abilities.

When we chafe under the leadership of controllers, these individuals short-circuit our creative abilities, leading to frustration and unproductivity. In response, many leave their jobs, searching for a place where people appreciate their contributions. Their departure leaves a void.

> Likewise, you younger people, submit yourselves to *your* elders. Yes, all of *you* be submissive to one another and be clothed with humility, for *"God resists the proud but gives grace to the humble."* —1 Peter 5:5

Points to Ponder

1. Have you served under a micromanager?

2. If so, what was the outcome?

3. Do you tend to micromanage?

4. If so, how can you begin loosening your grip and empowering others to use their creativity to accomplish the mission and vision?

Rebellious Workers or Church Members

Jesus faced this issue when He ministered among the first-century Jewish people. He certainly enjoyed a tremendous following from many grateful people whose lives He touched. But Christ struggled mightily against many of the religious leaders of the day. He grew frustrated with them. In Matthew 23:37-39, the Lord bared His heart toward those stubborn, rebellious people.

O Jerusalem, Jerusalem, the one who kills the prophets and stones those who are sent to her! How often I wanted to gather your children together, as a hen gathers her chicks under *her* wings, but you were not willing! See! Your house is left to you desolate; for I say to you, you shall see Me no more till you say, "Blessed *is* He who comes in the name of the LORD!"

What was the issue? Stubborn, rebellious people.

Moses, likewise, understood the difficulty of leading a rebellious people! The struggles he faced fill the pages of the Pentateuch. After the Lord demonstrated His unparalleled power through the ten plagues against Egypt and the parting of the Red Sea, the people continually carped about their situation. Their ultimate refusal to enter the Promised Land when they arrived at Kadesh Barnea (Numbers 13-14) resulted in a discipline that lasted forty years.

As a pastor, God blessed me with wonderful, cooperative Christ-followers. I thank the Lord for them. But, sprinkled through the ranks of each church, we would find one or two who resisted our leadership. Those individuals tended to keep my feet on the ground. Only in one church did I face a significant number of rebellious workers. Beth and I grew more in that church than in any place we served. But the offering of our service to God became excruciatingly painful. The good news is we grew! The Lord polished us in this crucible and removed some of our rough edges, a work He continues to do!

Points to Ponder

1. Have you experienced working with stubborn or rebellious people?

2. How did they impact you? The team?

3. Do you fall into the category of stubborn/rebellious? If so, what do you need to do to correct this bent?

Conflict Between the Pioneers and Homesteaders

He was a pastor in his forties when he moved to serve the next church—an experienced pastor who had a clearly defined philosophy of ministry.[39] By this time, he knew the direction this church needed to move to reach people for Christ. This pastor enjoyed successful turnarounds in his earlier ministries. He was

---

39   Brown, Penfold, Westra, *Pastor Unique*. This account is adapted from my previous work, *Pastor Unique: Becoming a Turnaround Leader*, 149-50.

excited by a new challenge at a church stuck in plateaued worship attendance for over twenty years. He also understood the pressing needs of the community—a community riddled with drug and alcohol addictions, broken families, dysfunctional adults and racial tensions. During the candidating process, the pastor asked the congregation, "Are you willing to do whatever we need to do to reach this community with the gospel?" The church responded with a resounding, "Yes, Pastor, yes!"

This capable pastor knew that major changes needed to happen. He hit the ground running, plunging right in, thinking the church was on board with him. The pastor took the church's word about reaching people for Christ. He misjudged the situation terribly. He felt his "charming" personality and persuasive abilities were enough! The church did not feel the same sense of urgency that compelled his previous church to make sweeping changes. He understood that he did not know how to lead this church in change. What worked in the "easy" churches did not work there.

Many existing members in this church gave lip service to reaching people, but their hearts did not follow. They did not see the fields "white unto harvest" (John 4:35). They viewed most outsiders as enemies, especially those different from them. Despite their passive-resistant behavior, the church grew fairly rapidly. So did the opposition to the new direction led by the pastor! The pioneers (old timers in the church) became unsettled when the homesteaders (the newbies) moved in and soon began to outnumber them.

After enjoying cohesiveness, unity, and relative calm in his previous ministries, the pastor became dismayed at the lack of unity that marred the new ministry. Nothing prepared him for the infighting and hostility exhibited by the believers in the church. He was not alone. Many of the pastors in the community experienced the same patterns of behavior, and the community itself reflected the same contentiousness.

Unfortunately, the community that desperately needed the gospel lost out because of the pioneers' cavalier attitude. After all, it was their church—it belonged to them! They forgot that the Lord Jesus Christ heads the church (Ephesians 1:22-23), and it belongs to Him.

Gene Wood, in his book *Leading Turn Around Churches*, describes the tensions between the pioneers and the homesteaders.

> The result is a range war. Who will control the land? A new pastor is more likely to identify with the homesteaders than the pioneers. He is usually anxious to move these newer people on the governing board and is likely to view the pioneers who hold the power as his adversaries.[40]

Many pastors run aground when they face this conflict between the pioneers and homesteaders. They are not trained in leading change and handling the attitudes of longtime members of these congregations. Business leaders in long-established businesses face the same pressures. I served in an engineering firm that experienced stability among the owners. Not long before I left the firm for full-time pastoral ministry, a new principal joined the company. I worked there for only a couple of years, but I felt the tension when this new principal arrived. He was a great guy, but everyone needed to kick the tires before we agreed he was okay!

The point: Challenges exist between the pioneers and the homesteaders. Be prepared!

---

40   Gene Wood, *Leading Turnaround Churches* (St. Charles: ChurchSmart, 2001), 49.

Points to Ponder

1. We all deal with people who are old-timers and new adds. How did this work in your situation?

2. Are you the pioneer? How did it feel when fresh people moved into your familiar territory? Did you feel threatened? Fearful?

3. Are you the homesteader? Did you feel welcomed or ostracized or have some other feelings when you arrived at a new place of worship or work?

4. How did you respond?

Poor Fit Between Leader and Company or Pastor and Church

Often, churches or businesses experience a disconnect between the leader and the organization. It may be a great church or a great company with capable and good leaders and people, but the two do not mesh. The leader and the church or business are both healthy; there is just a poor fit.

While I studied at Colorado State University, a New York City native moved to Fort Collins to study engineering. In his entire life, he never set foot outside the City. When he arrived at the old Stapleton airport in Denver, he hopped in a cab and said, "Take me to Fort Collins." The cabbie thought he was crazy. (The minimum wage in those days was $1.60). Sixty bucks later, he arrived at CSU. Don had never seen an open field or a cow. He said his face stayed glued to the window the entire trip. He told me later that he never returned to New York City. He adapted to his new environment. Think about placing Don in a small, rural community of 2,000 in rural America. There are bound to be challenges between Don and this vastly different environment.

A pastor moved to his first pastorate in a community of 3,000 after being actively involved in a church of 10,000 in a metropolitan area of eight million. You can imagine some of the rubs between the pastor and the congregation. Buying a pair of cowboy boots did not bridge the gap between the cultures. The pastor had great potential. The church was healthy, and the pastor was capable. The result of this union spelled disaster!

Points to Ponder

1. Can you think of a time when you were not a good fit for a job?

2. Can you think of others who did not fit well in their positions?

3. What are some possible courses of action to rectify these situations?

Bullies

Bullies cause untold damage in life. They personify conflict flashpoints. Their dominant personalities overwhelm their peers and often drive people into submission. Usually, bullies go unchecked because of the intimidation that characterizes them. Remember Diotrephes in 3 John 9. Here is another biblical example of a bully.

> Alexander the coppersmith did me much harm. May the Lord repay him according to his works. You also must beware of him, for he has greatly resisted our words. —2 Timothy 4:14-15

Suffice it to say at this point that bullies are tough. But we must not fear their wrath or intimidation. One of my friends says the best way to deal with a bully is to "punch them in the nose." He is saying that we must call their bluff.

We will say much more on this subject in Part 4.

Points to Ponder

1. Name some bullies you faced in your life. I can think of many, beginning with my childhood.

2. How have you dealt with bullies?

3. What is the result of inaction toward a bully?

Politics, Masks, Vax, and Government-Ordered Shutdowns

The adage, "Don't talk about politics or religion," has recently fallen on hard times. Political polarization has splintered families, churches, businesses and friendships in the past few years. The contentious elections go back further than 2020, but in 2020, political divisions came into sharp relief.

A ministry colleague had 25 families leave the church because this pastor did not reject the COVID-19 mask mandate outright. My colleague, Bud Brown, said to him, "Well, you're fortunate that you did not have to deal with this issue twenty-five times! You only had to deal with it once!" Others left the churches because their churches closed for a season. The challenge: Do you obey the government (Romans 13), or do you resist the wickedness of government as some see it?

These issues created cavernous divides in our culture—and they still do! How can we possibly deal with these deep-seated emotions that even lead to physical confrontations or even death?

A friend, Dr. John Craft, did his D.Min. dissertation on Ideologically Driven Differences (IDD) as they impact churches.[41] His conclusion is simple. We must focus on our mission and vision. We cannot let other issues drive a wedge between us. This approach can work in both businesses and churches. But it is "work!" We must focus on what draws us together (mission and vision) and not on what drives us apart.

Points to Ponder

1. How have the currently politically charged debates impacted you? Not just the presidential debates, but the debates in the church, your home and your workspace.

---

41   John M. Craft IV, "E Pluribus Una Ecclesia: Addressing Ideologically Driven Disunity Through a Multifaceted Approach" (Liberty University, 2023), Doctoral Dissertations and Projects, 4749. https://digitalcommons.liberty.edu/doctoral/4749/.

2. Have you suffered fractured relationships at work, in a church or a community organization?

3. Do these losses grieve you or anger you?

4. Can they be repaired? If so, how?

Assumptions and Unspoken Expectations

In 2020, part of our Advanced Pastoral Network team (formerly, TAP Inc.) traveled to a deeply conflicted church. While we did training on conflict management, a visiting denominational leader suggested that "assumptions" can lead to conflict. The more I pondered his statement, the more sense it makes.

All of us have assumptions. We assume that everyone else thinks just like we do. For example, churches often assume that the pastor will do the work of the ministry—all the work of the ministry. The pastor believes that he will have a reasonable work schedule and will enjoy sufficient time to spend with his family. These assumptions may not be compatible with one another.

A firm hires a new employee at what appears to be fair market value. The employee considers a forty-hour week to be standard. However, his boss assumes that his wage includes forty-five hours a week. When the employee checks out at five every afternoon, the unhappy boss demands more hours. The employee is disgruntled because he assumed that forty hours was sufficient. The unmet assumptions make for a difficult time for all the people involved.

A young pastor took a new position after being pushed out of his role as a youth leader. Three months later, the pastor at his new church fired him! The former youth pastor said, "Looking back, I saw several red flags I ignored." Desperate in his search, he ignored a good process of evaluating the new ministry opportunity.

In our first church, the trustees expected us to repair a broken space heater in the parsonage. We refused. Space heaters were deemed a health hazard. Second, I was not qualified to do the work. This encounter produced hard feelings.

Consequently, when we moved to our second church a few years later, I spent two and a half hours asking questions about the church and facilities. Then, the pulpit committee grilled me for another three hours concerning theological issues. When we finished the grill session, the pulpit committee and I greatly understood one another. This conversation led to a great ministry season.

A friend accepted the call to serve a church in upstate New York. When he arrived, the leadership told him that he needed to stoke the wood-burning furnace early on Sunday mornings. No one bothered to tell him during the candidating process that this was an expectation. The former pastors all took care of this chore, and the church expected my friend to do the same. My friend very firmly informed the church leaders that he would not take care of this task. Firing the furnace was not the reason he accepted the call. Never once did he fire the furnace in the years he served with the congregation.

A prime example of unmet expectations occurs in 1 Kings 12:1-14. Rehoboam ignored the advice of Solomon's advisors and followed the advice of his young friends. Rehoboam did not meet the expectations of the soon-to-be Northern Kingdom. The resulting rift between the Northern and Southern Kingdoms of Israel impacted the nation for centuries.

Points to Ponder

1. Describe a time when you made assumptions that disagreed with your employers' ideas.

2. Describe a time when your assumptions didn't match those of a friend or coworker.

Too often, people are so desperate for change that they paint a picture of themselves or their organization that leaves out significant facts and ignores the red flags. In this case, the best path forward is honest and sincere questioning. Before entering into a work agreement, ask lots of questions about expectations. Also, make certain that you make your wishes and expectations known.

Theological and Philosophical Differences

A few years ago, one of the leaders in the church I pastored said to me, "Gordon, we have two churches here. One is a grace church, and the other law." I immediately latched on to his statement. He nailed the challenges we faced. The smaller group was more Pharisaic and controlling, and the larger group was more grace-oriented. He made this statement just before we left that church. The rift became even more obvious when the church called its next senior pastor. When the associate pastor made a play to oust the new pastor, the new pastor fired the associate.

The associate eventually took about 80 people and started a new congregation. Looking back, I see that many of those 80 people created difficulties for us. What was the issue? I am grace-oriented; they were more legalistic and works-oriented.

We saw the same issue in one of the churches where I conducted an intervention. The pastor and his band of leaders were strict and demanding, while the majority of the church loved grace! The church nearly exploded in a ball of conflict. The pastor and all but one of the leadership team left. After their departure, harmony reigned once again. Those who left found other churches more suited to their theological position.

So, what kinds of theological or philosophical issues make for flashpoints of conflict? This list is suggestive but not complete!

- Grace Theology versus Lordship Salvation
- The Doctrine of Last Things
  - Amillennialism vs. Premillennialism
  - Replacement Theology (The church took Israel's place) vs. Dispensational Theology (God will use Israel again)
  - Pre, Mid or Post Tribulation Rapture
  - Dispensationalism vs. Covenant Theology
  - Open or closed communion or any communion at all
  - Believer's baptism versus infant baptism
- Leadership styles (elder rule) vs. congregational rule
- Music styles
- What Bible translation to use?
- Inward vs. outward focus on ministry
- Missional vs. attractional ministry
- Coffee in the auditorium vs "the sanctuary"
- Social Justice
- LGBTQ+

- Transgender issues
- Reliability of Scripture
- Role of women in ministry

In a business, the following may become issues.

- Controlling leadership vs. empowering leadership
- Innovative vs. traditional
- A firm that develops new leaders vs. a firm that gives no room for advancement
- Straight salary vs. profit sharing
- Most of the issues mentioned for churches

Once again, the best defense is to know where a church or a business stands on these and other issues before you become entwined in the work. Leaving a church or a business over these types of problems can be painful. Breaking fellowship with people you love leaves scars!

Points to Ponder

1. Which issues like these have impacted you (praise God if they have not)?

2. Can you name some other issues that divide people?

3. How did you handle the situation? Well? Poorly?

4. How do you plan to avoid similar challenges in the future?

Difficult People and Difficult Situations

Not all situations involve enemies or extremely difficult people. Sometimes, we must deal with difficult situations. Barb Ayers, who served together in ministry for decades with her pastor-husband Duane, related this story to me, and it stuck.

Joe and Mary were ranchers who lived in a sparsely settled area, so they didn't have many visitors.

One day, just at noon, as Mary was setting dinner on the table, there was a knock at the back door. There stood Ed and Sally Bitterly, neighbors on their way back to their ranch. They decided to stop and say hello.

"Come in. We are just ready to sit down to dinner. I'll set a couple more places," said Mary. They ate, visited, and compared hay and cattle prices, and the women caught up on "womanly" news. As Joe and Mary headed for bed, they commented on how nice it was for Ed and Sally to stop. Joe had heard rumors that the Bitterlys were a bit shiftless but didn't mention it to Mary.

Again, one noon, there was a knock at the door. Again, the Bitterlys were invited in. As before, the four visited, and when it was time to clean up, Ed and Sally suddenly needed to leave for home. It was interesting how the Bitterlys began to stop more often just at mealtime and, just as interesting, how they always had "to get home" just as it was time to clean up. This went on for a time.

One noon, Ed and Sally arrived as usual. The four of them visited, but as they finished the meal, Mary opened the screen door for Shep, their dog, to enter. Methodically, she took each plate and put it on the floor so that Shep could lick it clean. As Shep "washed" each plate, Mary picked it up, checked to see if it was clean and stacked it in the cupboard. One by one, Shep licked the plates clean, and one by one, Mary put them in the cupboard.

Need I even mention—the Bitterlys never stopped by for a meal again![42]

Not every situation is as easily handled as this one. But all of us face issues with very draining people (VDPs) or, as some would describe them, Extra Grace Required (EGRs). Sometimes, it's a coworker, a nosy neighbor, or an annoying aunt or uncle. Regardless, we must learn how to handle the "Bitterlys" in our lives.

Most people tend to be passive or evasive with such individuals. The problem with these approaches is that the issues are never resolved. Do you need to "break the sound barrier" with them and actually name the difficulties they cause you? (I define breaking the sound barrier in Part 3).

Misunderstanding

A friend of mine added "Misunderstanding" to the list of Flash Points. When most of us experience conflict with someone, we tend to take it personally and think it is about us. In some cases, it is not about us! There are many reasons people have conflict, and it may have nothing to do with us. Personal issues, personal struggles, and other challenges may impact the conflict.

My friend worked for a large division in a large corporation. He noticed an increased amount of gossip among his charges. He finally said, "Where is the source of this gossip?" His workers said, "It's you!" He angrily responded, "Me! How can it be me? I've never shared one shred of gossip."

His employees said, "Yes, but you've really been on edge lately. We feel that corporate is going to sell off our division from the company! Your attitude convinced us of this reality!" No wonder the employees were on edge!

My friend opened up to them. "Listen, this has nothing to do with our company or our division. My father had a stroke. He lives 400 miles away, and I'm his only child. I'm in a quandary because I don't know what to do. That's why I've been operating with a short fuse. This issue has nothing to do with you or the company. It's about my father and me!"

The world is a big place, and not everything revolves around us. When conflict occurs, be sure to understand all the dynamics involved.

Money

Money and its trusty sidekick, greed, ruin many families, friendships and relationships. This pair shows up in limitless ways. Here's an example from Jesus' life in Luke 12:13-15.

> "Teacher, tell my brother to divide the inheritance with me." But He said to him, "Man, who made Me a judge or an arbitrator over you?" And He said to them, "Take heed and beware of covetousness, for one's life does not consist in the abundance of the things he possesses."

Settling estates produces many broken relationships. In the division of the Promised Land, Israel cast lots to determine which tribe inherited which portion (Numbers 33:54). This eliminated arguments over the land. Some families do the same. They draw straws to see which portion of the estate falls to each part of the family.

In terms of personal finances, families often disagree over how to allocate their limited resources. Children may quibble over who received the most Christmas presents. Many divorces arise from conflicts over the use of money. Business partners separate because they cannot agree on a financial path forward. The bottom line is the bottom line!

Jesus' words ring true. "Life does not consist in the abundance of the things we possess." Live above the financial din by focusing on Christ and His Kingdom (Matthew 6:33). Your mind and your body will appreciate this focus. So will friends and family!

Points to Ponder

1. When have finances become an issue in your relationships?

2. How did this impact you and those around you?

3. Do you need to mend some financial fences?

Other Flash Points

I've observed these flashpoints over the years. Every time I train on conflict resolution and biblical peacemaking, I discover new challenges that people and churches face. What are some other challenges you confront? Please send me your thoughts via the email at the back of the book. I would love to hear from you!

Points to Ponder

1. Which flashpoints of conflict affect you most?

2. In your spiritual relationships (church)?

3. In secular relationships?

4. Do you have some "Bitterlys" in your life? Can you identify them?

5. How might you creatively deal with the challenges these EGR people require?

6. How have you contributed to this untenable situation?

PART 3

The Practice of Peacemaking

- ► BREAK THE SOUND BARRIER
- ► THE OBJECTIVES OF PEACEMAKING
- ► ESSENTIAL KEYS FOR MENDING FENCES

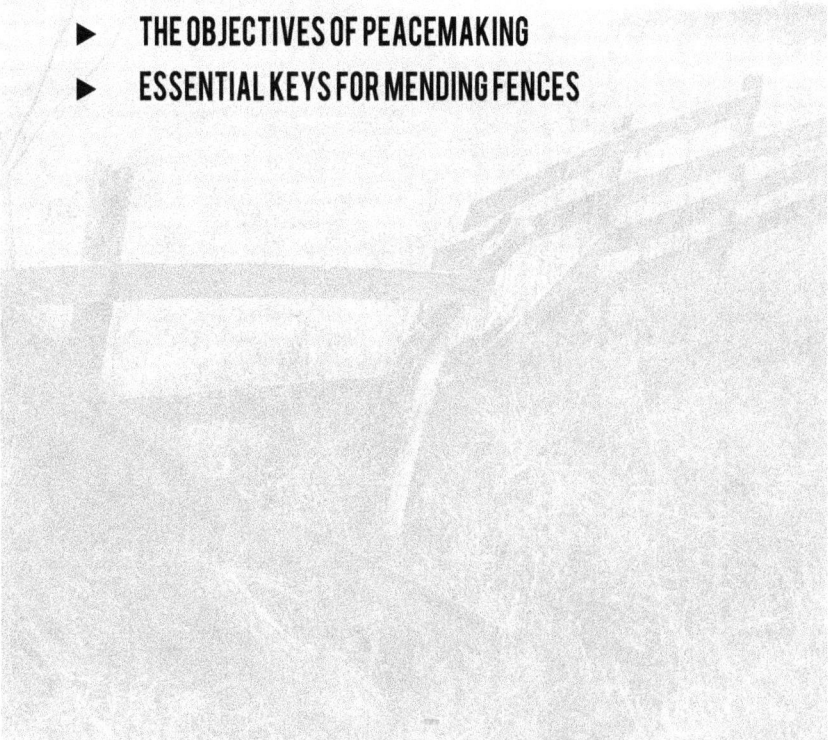

CHAPTER 8

BREAK THE SOUND BARRIER

For some, peacemaking is a breeze. However, for most people, the thought of dealing with those who have harmed us or those with whom we have issues terrifies us! Many find the idea of conflict paralyzing! Unresolved conflict affects people just like leeches—it sucks the life blood right out of us!

In this section, we will examine key practices essential for pursuing peace. First, we must talk about breaking the sound barrier. Most people will not speak up in the face of conflict, resulting in difficulties that linger and divide. Second, we must clearly understand the objectives of peacemaking. Third, we must not overlook the essential keys to mending fences! Fourth, we must recognize that vertical forgiveness between God and us demands horizontal forgiveness, forgiveness on the level between others and us.

One of the greatest challenges people confront in the face of conflict is silence. People would rather suffer in silence than enjoy the freedom of release from the clutches of conflict.

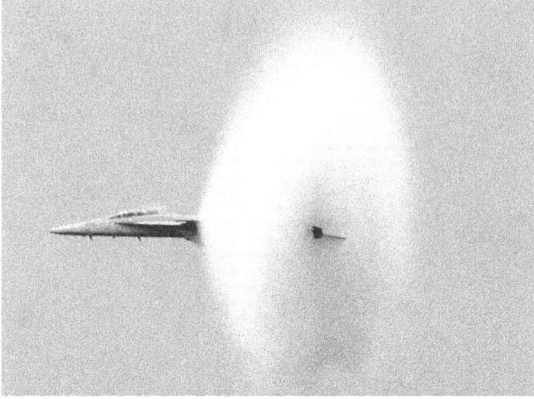

Figure 4

This is a photograph of a plane breaking the sound barrier.[43] Notice the aircraft seems to be breaking through a fog. This phenomenon occurs when a plane passes the speed of sound. I want to challenge you and your church, civic group or business to break the sound barrier in conflict communication. When believers open up to speak the truth in love, they, too, will move through the fog and into freedom! Unfortunately, Christ-followers are silent more often than not.

As we continue, we want to unpack challenges and solutions for mending fences by breaking the sound barrier.

- **The Silence of the Lambs**
- **The Deceitful Causes of Silence**
- **Consequences of Passivity and Evasiveness**
- **God's Solution to Passivity and Evasiveness**

The Silence of the Lambs

Multiple issues challenge individuals and groups in conflict. Two issues, in particular, lurk just beneath the surface: gossip

---

43   Photograph, https://cdn.pixabay.com/photo/2013/04/03/01/46/breaking-the-sound-barrier-99684_960_720.jpg. ACCESSED December 7, 2024.

and silence. Both involve the tongue. Gossip always wins the black ribbon! However, gossip has a sinister sister—silence! People need to bleat in the face of mistreatment! All too often, they remain silent when encountering conflict! I want to invite churches, believers and individuals in general to break the sound barrier, to break the stranglehold of conflict that, like a python, squeezes the very life out of churches, families, marriages and work relationships.

I've discovered that silence, the inability or fear of speaking out during a conflict situation, hampers conflict resolution. What do I mean by this statement? Frequently, believers who **should** speak out in a conflicted situation hold their tongues. In so doing, they add to the damage inflicted on a church body, family and work relationships, businesses, civic groups and friends. Open channels of communication produce vitality, while silence breeds internal rot!

Here is a statement from one member of a conflicted church that speaks volumes about the sin of silence! "I'm so thankful for the conflict intervention team. Everyone in the church knew we had problems, but no one talked about them! Once we voted for the intervention, it was like the dam burst, and now we can openly talk about those things that have been **suffocating** us for the **past twenty years!**" (emphasis added). In this case, an invitation to a conflict intervention team ignited the conversation. What will it take to ignite constructive conversation in your church or among your relationships?

The Deceitful Causes of Silence

Why do we fail to communicate amid conflict? What causes spiritual lockjaw? Passivity and evasiveness contribute mightily to the malignancy of unresolved conflict. These conflict response styles are often as destructive as gossip! One reason people avoid conflict is we prefer to avoid open conflict in a group. Rather, we wish to maintain homeostasis and allow bullies and strong personalities to run roughshod over us and others rather than dealing openly with destructive issues. Consequently, we sweep the uncomfortable under the rug and suffer in silence.

As we survey conflicted churches, we consistently find that about 85-90% of believers who attend these churches exhibit passive or evasive behaviors when responding to conflict! These percentages will be similar in other groups. These response styles prevent people from proactively dealing with conflict issues.

Passive people fear dealing openly with real issues. Conflict causes them great pain and tremendous anxiety. Rather than face the reality of what they perceive as more significant pain in facing conflict, they justify their passivity using skewed logic. They reason, "I will just let this issue pass. Jesus said that we are supposed to love one another. So, in the name of love, I'll just let this infraction pass." When another believer walks all over these doormats, they think, "I will love my brother (or sister) the way Jesus asked me to love him or her." Consequently, passive people often become the punching bags for church bullies. Self-preservation, not love, motivates them.

Evasive individuals see trouble coming and do everything they can to avoid it. I have used this defense mechanism myself. For example, when serving in my first church, I always avoided one particular individual early on Sunday mornings. Why? Because this man could deflate my spiritual balloon faster than anyone I have ever met. And I was not alone! I did not avoid him the rest of the week, but I did my best not to see him before our Sunday morning service because I knew he could destroy my frame of mind. Ultimately, I went to his home to deal with a negative issue affecting the entire church! I presented him with three options: 1) Go to another church where he could be "happy," 2) change his attitude, or 3) continue to be miserable and make everyone around him miserable. He chose the third option! Today, I would handle the problem differently. For the sake of the gospel, I would only give him the first two options! I would not allow him to continue in his sin!

Another manifestation of evasiveness is the proverbial "cold shoulder." This behavior occurs when we "write off" those who cause us distress. After all, a cold shoulder is better than a pain in the neck!

Consequences of Passivity and Evasiveness

What are some of the consequences of passive and evasive behavior? Two immediately come to mind: the **time bomb** and **divorce**.

Individuals allow issues to remain unresolved. Resentment builds like a festering splinter. Eventually and inevitably, an explosion erupts. The consequence for the church, the place of business and the civic club: Carnage!—Shouting matches or even fisticuffs. The testimony of the Lord suffers another blow! Many mass shooters fail to deal with their inner frustrations and attack others while blaming them for their failure to address these issues. Stephen Paddock killed 60 and wounded at least 413 others in Las Vegas. He became a ticking time bomb.

The FBI released documents in 2023 that suggested Paddock was motivated by a desire to exact revenge on the casinos for the losses he had incurred. The documents also revealed that Paddock had been planning the attack for months and had stockpiled weapons and ammunition in his hotel room.[44]

---

44   https://search.brave.com/search?q=las+vegas+shooter&source=desktop, accessed May 1, 2024.

This fruit of people stuffing their feelings inside impacts anyone on the receiving end of such behavior. Please break the sound barrier.

Second: **divorce.** The results will be similar to the results found in a marriage where one of the marriage partners abuses the other. Without warning or discussion, the abused partner walks out, never to return! This consequence repeats itself all too frequently in marriages, churches and service organizations at every level of society; individuals disappear, never to return to your church, work or organization. Unfortunately, many of these individuals never return, period. Their evasiveness becomes permanent.

God's Solutions for Passivity and Evasiveness

Interestingly, the solution to the problem lies within the grasp of every conflicted person! God desires each of us to maintain good relationships with others. In churches, He yearns that each of us "speaking the truth in love, may grow up in all things into Him who is the head—Christ— from whom the whole body, joined and knit together by what every joint supplies, according to the effective working by which every part does its share, causes growth of the body for the edifying of itself in love" (Ephesians 4:15-16). The initial step requires us to speak the truth in love. No soft soap. No tap dancing. Face the issue. Speak the truth in love. Spiritual growth is the inevitable byproduct of such action! Consider the following story.

A very contentious woman moved into a quiet neighborhood. She spoke with a thick accent and was rude and abrasive with everyone she met (at least, that was everyone's perception). We'll nickname her "Anna the Hun." Anna's next-door neighbor, a Christian woman, was so intimidated by this harsh woman that she no longer worked in her yard. She became so anxious about cantankerous Anna that she would peek out the window before getting into her car (she parked her car in the driveway between the two houses). If the coast were clear, she would sprint to her car, palms sweating, fumble to put the key in the ignition, fire up the engine, and race away. She was petrified—and avoiding.

Finally, she prayed, saying, "Lord, this is ridiculous. I'm a self-made prisoner in my own house. Please give me the courage to face my fears and to face my neighbor." At that point, she decided to bake a pie and take it over to Anna. She baked and prayed. Before the pie and her resolve completely cooled, she strode out the front door, down the sidewalk and knocked on the door. She secretly hoped that Anna would not be home. The door opened, and she sputtered out the words, "Hi! I've baked this pie especially for you." She was shocked and somewhat mortified when Anna invited her into her home. As they visited and ate pie together, Anna poured out her heart. It turned out that she was lonely, felt totally like an outsider, and had no friends (no surprise here!). That day, a special friendship was born because a believer finally decided to **Break the Sound Barrier**! Freedom followed!

Are there times when silence is preferred? Of course. If the issues are not overwhelming and we can forgive them, we must (1 Peter 4:8, Proverbs 10:12-13, and Proverbs 19:11). However, when the sinful actions of others damage us and others, we dare not keep silent!

Points to Ponder

1. How do you tend to handle conflict? I recommend that you purchase "Conflict Style Assessment"[45] from NextStep Resources. This tool raises people's awareness of their conflict management style. I tend to be evasive

---

45   Jim Van Yperen, "Conflict Style Assessment" (Apple Valley MN, NextStep Resources) n.d.

and defensive—both inappropriate ways to handle conflict. I now recognize my default mechanisms and adjust my approach to conflict better than in the past.

2. What will you need to do to break the sound barrier in your own life, in your church, with interpersonal relationships? You may be one of the 85% of those who are passive and evasive. Perhaps you need to:

- Recognize areas of unresolved conflict in your own life.
- Recognize your false "love." Real love faces reality and deals with it.
- Identify the cause(s) of the conflict.
- Ask God for courage and wisdom to do what is right.
- Suppose you are the cause of the problem. Practice the truth of Matthew 5:23-24. Own your part of the controversy.
- If someone has sinned against you, then own your part in bringing reconciliation. Carefully follow the process outlined in Matthew 18:15-18. We will unpack these passages in Part 4 of the book.

CHAPTER 9

THE OBJECTIVES OF MENDING FENCES[46]

When we discuss peacemaking and biblical conflict resolution, we must first understand foundational assumptions. Second, we must clearly understand the objectives of conflict resolution. Third, we must clearly understand the expectations of the peacemaking process, including the dismissal of unrepentant individuals from the congregation or the dismissal of employees or community group members who persistently create conflict. In the event of failure to achieve repentance, confession and forgiveness, the offending parties must be dismissed until these biblical responses take place.

Note: Churches possess an edge when dealing with sin and unrepentant members because the prescriptions of the Word of God carry great weight. The problems at work or with other groups may not be simple, but the basic principles apply but may not be used with the same level of authority. By all means, deal with issues as you attempt to mend broken relationships.

---

46   Much of the material in this section is adapted from Chapter 8 in my previous work in *Pastor Unique: Becoming a Turnaround Leader.*

Here are some foundational assumptions. First, Christ desires harmony in the local church.

> I, therefore, the prisoner of the Lord, beseech you to walk worthy of the calling with which you were called, with all lowliness and gentleness, with longsuffering, bearing with one another in love, endeavoring to keep the unity of the Spirit in the bond of peace. —Ephesians 4:1

A large part of our service to the Savior is maintaining unity in the church.

Second, the primary objective of peacemaking is the restoration of broken relationships. As we survey numerous texts related to peacemaking, this objective screams from the pages of the Bible. Of course, the first relationship requiring mending is between people and the Lord. "Be reconciled to God" (2 Corinthians 5:20).

Vindictive, hateful responses find no place in biblical conflict resolution. Our attitude must not be, "Throw the bum out!" Our ego may take a hit, and we desire to respond in anger by striking back. The motive for dealing with an issue becomes more about protecting our reputation rather than restoring an erring person. I remember reading about a church in Oklahoma City in the early 1980s that excommunicated a woman for an offense. The church appeared to use discipline correctly. However, the church inappropriately published a notice in the newspaper declaring that the woman had been cast out. She sued the church for libel and won a judgment for $600,000! That was real money in 1980!

As a first step, our response must always align with 1 Peter 4:8, "Above all, keep loving one another earnestly, since love covers a multitude of sins." Most offenses are trivial and easily forgiven. We must possess an attitude that seeks forgiveness and reconciliation. As long as no long-term damage occurs, or you do not experience deep wounds or people persist in bad behaviors, commit the offense to the Lord and move on. But, if an offense comes to mind every time you see the offender, you have not forgiven them. You must then take the needed steps to reconcile.

Second, you must follow the biblical mandates to resolve the issue. If repentance is not forthcoming and reconciliation is not possible, the church must stand fast in fidelity to its Head, our Lord and Savior, Jesus Christ. The offending parties must be dismissed from the fellowship until biblical responses take place.

CHAPTER 10

ESSENTIAL KEYS FOR MENDING FENCES

When the conflict bug bites, we should observe the following guidelines and apply these principles and processes in our conflict resolution toolbox. The implications of applying these truths bear great weight in successful conflict resolution and peacemaking. Please do not ignore the bedrock essentials for success in mending fences.

1. **Keep the circle small!** By that, I mean that the people directly involved in the conflict situation are the only ones who need to know about the issue. Involving others in problems that are not their own destroys ministries, relationships and lives. It used to be that gossip traveled at the speed of sound. Now, gossip travels at the speed of light! Today, the threat of rumors, gossip, and picking sides is accelerated by the use of social media, the internet, and the ease of sending messages, all at the speed of light! People can instantly invite their friends into the fray. God's counsel to all of this is to stay out of the dispute unless you are directly involved.

Our natural inclination is to rally the troops to our cause. Godly counsel says no to that bent in our nature.

2. **Own your own.** One key to settling difficulties between individuals requires people to own their own part of the problem. Conflict is rarely a one-way street. Godly individuals recognize and repent of their contribution to the issue.

3. **Apply the proper passages to the conflict issue at hand and the appropriate responses to each.** Note in your mind: Matthew 18:15-18 is not the conflict resolution catchall. Every issue invokes a particular passage and carries a specific prescription. Search the scriptures and this volume to apply the correct prescription to a conflict problem.

4. **You know, you go!** This means that those who see and understand a problem must be the ones who involve themselves in the resolution. A believer cannot be one to pass the buck or to stand passively in the face of difficulty. Many church people bury their heads in the sand while church bullies and strong-willed people destroy churches and ministries.

PART 4

Major Conflict Passages and Prescriptions for Mending Fences

► MAJOR CONCEPTS FOR MENDING FENCES
► CHURCH AND CLERGY KILLERS

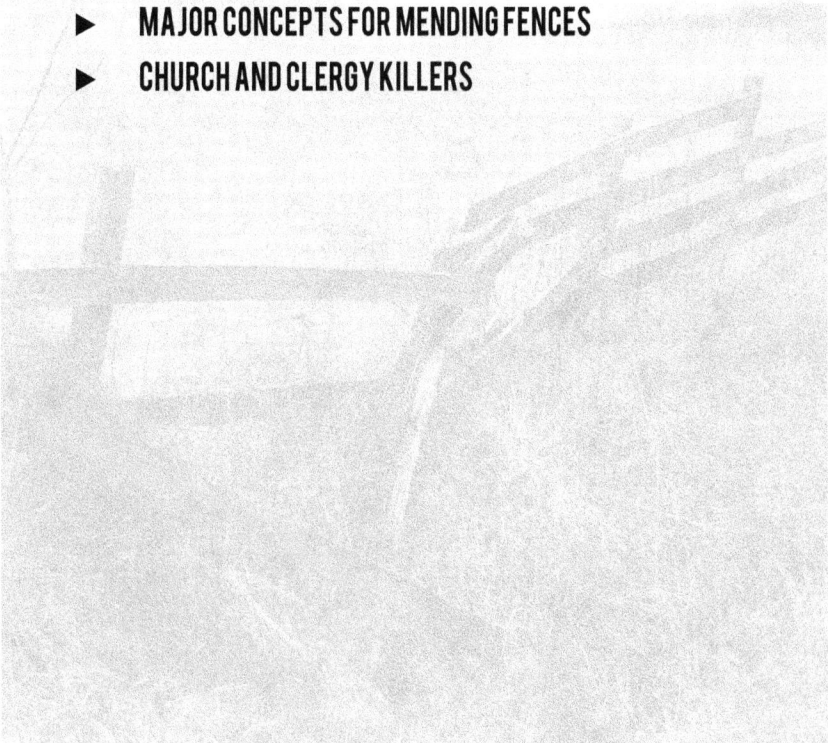

CHAPTER 11

MAJOR CONCEPTS FOR MENDING FENCES

Please note that the passages cited in Chapter 11 apply to Christ-followers and local churches. Many of the principles translate into other areas, such as work relationships, family relationships, friends, and dealing with neighbors. As we live and breathe in a world racked by constant conflict, it is okay to apply these principles to our own lives. You must realize that you may not have the same boundaries that churches offer in conflict resolution. However, if you apply these principles and resources to life outside the church, you may be pleasantly surprised by the outcomes. Know that not everyone desires to play by the "rules." Therefore, do not be surprised if people resist your overtures of peace! Here is a look at the major chapter divisions.

We will look at eight biblical issues that require people to address conflict resolution in significantly different areas. In addition, we will address the problem of gossip. Each passage we cite addresses a specific situation, and we should apply only this text to that particular conflict initiator when that problem is the challenge. Each of these problems demands a different approach and a different prescription for the difficulties involved.

Sometimes, people offend others either intentionally or unintentionally. On occasion, others sin against us. How must we handle civil lawsuits between church members? What must we do when someone is caught in a trespass? How must we respond to false teaching or to those who persist in using slanderous or abusive speech? What should happen to a leader who continually sins or abuses those under their care? We also face people who love to divide groups and drive wedges between people. How must we respond to them? Finally, gossip is a terrible blight on any group as it damages relationships and destroys lives. How can we firmly deal with gossip in our circles?

- **My Offense Against Another**
- **Another's Offense Against Me**
- **Civil Lawsuits in the Church**
- **A Fellow Believer is Caught in a Trespass**
- **A Disorderly Brother**
- **Sexual Immorality in the Church**
- **False Teaching and Blasphemous Speech**
- **Discipline for a Sinful Leader**
- **Dealing with Divisive People**
- **Stopping Gossip Dead in Its Tracks**

My Offense Against Another

Matthew 5:21-26

Gordon occasionally puts his foot in his mouth (that's saying something as he wears a size 15 shoe!). I have created many opportunities to practice the principles of this passage. The good news is that I am much more discerning than in times past and taste shoe leather less frequently.

Early in my first pastorate, I had serious back trouble that my doctor treated with a prescribed muscle relaxant. I went to a

Wednesday evening Bible study after taking one of the tablets. During the study, I asked a series of questions. One dear lady answered nearly every time. I noticed her Bible had been published with pencil sketches to illustrate various passages. With my "relaxed" tongue, I said, "Geneva, I know why you have all the answers. It's because your Bible has pictures in it!"

On the way home, I realized how offensive that statement sounded. I immediately called her to apologize. She graciously replied, "I don't even remember that, and if I did, it wouldn't be a problem." I'm thankful for her gracious response. It could have been much different! On other occasions, I did hurt someone. Recognition and quick action on my part averted more than one potential disaster.

When these issues arise, deal with them summarily for the health of the body of Christ, for your testimony and your health. Remember, **keep the circle small; own your own; you know, you go!**

Matthew 5:21-26	
The Problem	A believer realizes they have offended another believer
The Parties Involved	Two people: the offender and the presumed offended
The Problem Solver	The offender
The Process	1. When you are on your way to worship and remember an offfense committed by you against another, leave your offering. Note reconciliation trumps giving! 2. Seek out the one you offended and seek forgiveness
The Purpose	Reconciliation
The Result	Reconciliation and harmony

Figure 5

165

Points to Ponder

1. Have you injured another party?

2. How did you respond to the situation? Flight? Ignore the difficulty? Seek forgiveness?

3. How did the episode turn out?

Another's Offense Against Me
Matthew 18:15-18

In churches, a believer may sin against (harm) another believer.[47] The offense may be real or imagined. In either case, this passage must be invoked to produce harmony in the fellowship. The objective is always reconciliation. The process is crucial. First, the offended person goes to the offender alone. **(Remember to keep the circle small!)** If they fail to reconcile, the offended one takes two or three witnesses to verify the facts (enlarge the circle slightly). If reconciliation fails to occur, the issue is brought to the church. Most of the time, people use Matthew 18:15-17 for church discipline. That is, if the parties fail to reconcile in this third step, the offending person is dismissed from the assembly.

---

47   A textual problem exists in this passage. The purpose of this book is not to share exegetical textual criticism, but this variant reading carries great weight in this text. Two of the oldest manuscripts read, "If a brother sins," while the vast majority of manuscript evidence supports the text, "If a brother sins against you." (Greek– εἰς σε [eis se]). Textual criticism, the art and science of weighing thousands of manuscripts to ascertain the correct reading of a passage, is challenging at best. In this case, the two oldest complete manuscripts, Aleph and B (Vaticanus), support the omission of the phrase "against you." However, the vast majority of the evidence, including other Alexandrian and other text types, include this phrase (these texts include D, K, L X, D Q P. The UBS and NA 27 bracket this phrase, calling the validity of the phrase into question. The NKJV and ESV include the phrase, while the NASB 1995, NIV, and NET translations omit the phrase. So, scholars remain divided. Added to this argument for including this phrase as original is Peter's question in Matthew 18:21, "Then Peter came to Him and said, 'Lord, how often shall my brother sin against me (Greek—εἰς ἐμὲ [eis eme]), and I forgive him? Up to seven times?'" Peter evidently understood that Jesus was speaking of a brother sinning against him (the majority reading). It seems that the internal evidence (the flow of the text) and the vast majority of the presence of this reading favor including this phrase. Therefore, without going into greater depth, I will use the phrase "against you" as original. Including "brother" in the text is how Peter understood Jesus' admonition.

However, my friend, Dr. Steve Smith,[48] pointed out an extraordinary bit of Greek grammar that is often missed that impacts the application of this passage. In Matt 18:17, the text reads, "let him be to you (second person, **singular** in Greek), like a heathen and a tax collector," which shows that the objective of this process is reconciliation between the offender and the one offended. This has nothing to do with fellowship with others in the body of Christ. The text that follows in Matthew 18:21-35 points out the essential need for forgiveness between two fellow believers. Churches must take care to be equitable in these conflict situations. Should the issue affect many in the church, discipline may be in order. Otherwise, the reconciliation issue remains between the offender and the offended.

Matthew 18:15-18

The Problem	A believer has sinned against another believer
The Parties Involved	The offender and the one offended
The Problem Solver	The offender and the one offended (initially). If the two cannot reconcile, the offended takes two or three witnesses. If this does not produce reconciliation, the whole church is included.
The Process	The offended seeks the offender to attempt reconciliation. If that fails, the offended takes several witnesses to observe the attempt at reconciliation. If the offender remains unrepentant, the offender comes before the church. If there is no reconciliation, the offender is treated as an unbeliever and a tax collector.
The Purpose	Reconciliation
The Result	Reconciliation or the estrangement between the offender and the offended occurs after all efforts for reconciliation fail

Figure 6

---

48   Dr. Steve Smith, personal conversation, May 1, 2025. Used by permission.

Points to Ponder:

1. Have people injured you intentionally or unintentionally?

2. How did you respond? Fight? Flight? Freeze? Invoke Matthew 18:15-18?

3. What outcomes took place?

4. Have you injured another believer?

5. How did you respond to their overtures for reconciliation?

6. Are you sleeping well?

Civil Lawsuits in the Church
1 Corinthians 6:1-11

Occasionally, personal difficulties or disagreements produce such anger and hostility that believers go to court to battle against one another. The text of 1 Corinthians 6:1-11 gives the path to follow when this happens. Please note that this passage does not speak about **criminal matters but civil matters only**. Building projects and church relocation often become heated issues, and the need may arise for a biblical settlement in the matter. Challenges relating to business, lending money, and a host of other human interactions often push people to the breaking point. They feel their only recourse is to take their opponent to court. This passage offers God's prescription for settling these types of problems **in the church**. An older TV show with Judge Wapner states, "Don't take matters into your own hands. Take them to court." Poor advice for believers seriously at odds with one another.

The verse in 1 Corinthians 6:4 may be read as a question or as an imperative. Vincent describes the passage's interpretive dilemma.

> Seat them as judges on the tribunal. It is disputed whether appoint (Greek— kathizete) is to be taken as imperative, set (A. V.[Authorized Version—King James Bible]), or as interrogative, do ye set (Rev.).* The A. V. seems, on the whole, preferable. The passage is well paraphrased by Farrar. "Dare they, the destined judges of the world and of angels, go to law about mere earthly trifles, and that before the heathen? Why did they not rather set up the very humblest members of the Church to act as judges in such matters? [49]

If the verb "appoint" (Greek—kathizete) is indicative and thus a question, the answer is "no." Pick the most esteemed in the church to hear the case." If it's an imperative, then the command is to place the lowliest member over the proceedings. Either option fits the flow of the passage. My inclination is toward putting the most esteemed in the church body to hear the case, but the other option fits well with the future position of the saints. The Lord posits two better alternatives to the contrary contestants in verse 7. First, allow oneself to take wrong (Greek, ἀδικεῖσθε) rather than suffer the defeat in the matter of love. Second, allow oneself to be cheated rather than damage the name of Christ. These responses reflect an attitude of humility rather than the self-seeking of the courtroom!

---

49   Marvin R. Vincent, *Word Studies in the New Testament*, Vol. 3 (New York: Charles Scribner's Sons, 1887) 106.

I spoke about this problem in a church in Makeevka, Ukraine, in 1996. Three issues rose to the surface in the church that became flashpoints of division. In all three cases, at least one of the parties threatened to go to court for a settlement. In one situation, a believing contractor did some work on another believer's home. When the contractor completed the work, he presented a bill to the homeowner. The owner said to the contractor, "You did a terrible job. I refuse to pay you." The contractor replied, "There is not one square corner or one plumb wall in your whole house. I did the best I could, given the state of your house. Pay up!" Who is right? What would be a just settlement? This passage in 1 Corinthians 6:1-11 gives biblical guidance for such cases. Whatever we do, let's not bring shame on the Name of our Lord Jesus!

Here's a classic illustration of 1 Corinthians 6:1-11 in action from the pen of biblical expositor, H. A. Ironside.

Many years ago, as a little fellow, I attended a meeting in Toronto where some difficulty had come up between brethren, and they did as the apostle suggests. My dear mother took me along. ... I well remember how horrified I was to see men I esteemed and had been taught to respect apparently so indignant with each other. I can remember one man springing to his feet and with clenched fists saying, "I will put up with a good deal, but one thing I will not put up with. I will not allow you to put anything over on me; I will have my rights!" An old Scotch brother who was rather hard of hearing leaned forward, holding his ear and said, "What was that, brother? I did not get that!" "I say, I will have my rights," said the man. "But you did not mean that, did you? Your rights? If you had your rights, you would be in hell, wouldn't you? And you are forgetting–aren't you? – that Jesus did not come to get his rights. He came to get His wrongs, and He got them." I can still see that man standing there for a moment like one transfixed, and then the tears broke from his eyes, and he said, "Brethren, I have been all wrong. Handle the case as you think best," and he sat down and put his face in his hands and sobbed before the Lord, and everything was settled in three minutes. When in this spirit, it is so easy to clear things up; when we bow before the Lord. He straightens them out.[50]

Such is the simplicity of following the Lord's outline for civil issues that divide believers.

1 Corinthians 6:1-11	
The Problem	One believer has sued another before the court in a civil matter
The Parties Involved	The plaintiff, the defendant, and the church
The Problem Solver	The church and the two contestants
The Process	1. Recognize the church's position. In this case, the Lord reminds believers that believers will judge angels and the world (2-3). If we can handle those responsibilities in the future, He reminds us that we can deal with the "trivial" in our current lives!
	2. Hold a "trial" in the church
	3. Appoint the "least" (or most esteemed) believer in the church as a "judge"
	4. Take the loss and walk away
The Purpose	1. The Lord is treated with respect
	2. The issue dividing the two is settled
The Result	1. The issue is settled
	2. The name of Christ is honored
	3. Those outside the church will notice

Figure 7

---

50   H. A. Ironside, *1 and 2 Corinthians*, reprint of 1938 edition (Grand Rapids, Kregel Publications, 2006), 106

Points to Ponder

1. Have you observed a time when two believers went to court over a civil matter?

2. What was the outcome?

3. How should these individuals handle their disagreement?

A Fellow Believer is Caught in a Trespass

Galatians 6:1 & 10

In Galatians 6:1, 10, the Lord instructs us on how we should treat a fellow believer who is caught in a fault, a sinful behavior.

> Brethren, if a man is overtaken in any trespass, you who *are* spiritual restore such a one in a spirit of gentleness, considering yourself lest you also be tempted. ... Therefore, as we have opportunity, let us do good to all, especially to those who are of the household of faith. —Galatians 6:1, 10

In this scenario, a believer is overtaken (detected, caught red-handed, or surprised) in a fault (false step, transgression or sin). The one who sees someone in a misstep must go to the church leadership (those who are spiritual) with the problem. The leadership, first, must prepare themselves lest they find themselves tempted. Then they approach the offender with gentleness. Some leaders may become domineering or unforgiving. The Lord warns against both attitudes.

Here is an illustration of how one church handled a particularly thorny situation. One of the church members worked for the county government. Someone discovered that his county computer contained pornographic material, an infraction for a county employee. They caught him with his hand in the proverbial cookie jar. Since he worked for a public agency, his fault hit the newspaper. Nearly everyone in the community and the church knew the situation. How was the church to handle this?

The church leadership met with him. He confessed his sin before them with tears. He then came before the church body and humbly repented for his actions.

In discussing a plan to move forward, the leadership said, "We know this man is not the only man in our community to have a problem with pornography. So, the church brought in Bill Perkins, a leader who helped many escape the clutches of addiction to porn. (His book, *Six Battles Every Man Must Win*, is a great resource for all who struggle in this area). The church ran about 150 in worship attendance at the time. Over 200 men from the church and community showed up for their meeting with Bill Perkins.

This account is a great example of how believers and churches can act redemptively towards those caught in a transgression. This example is Galatians 6:1, 10 at its best!

Galatians 6:1, 10

The Problem	A believer is overtaken (detected, caught red-handed, surprised) in a fault (false step, transgression, sin)
The Parties Involved	The observer, the spiritual ones and the one overtaken in a fault
The Problem Solver	The observer and those who are spiritual
The Process	1. The observation and report 2. Spiritual preparation 3. Gently approaching the guilty party 4. Restoration or removal in the event of unrepentance
The Purpose	Restoration to fruitful Christian living
The Result	1. Restoration 2. Removal from the church if there is no repentance

Figure 8

Points to Ponder

1. What natural inclinations do you display when you observe a transgression in another?

2. Ignore the issue?

3. Feel judgmental?

4. Gossip and tell your friends?

5. Consider how the Lord would have you handle a situation that will honor Him and rescue a needy individual.

A Disorderly Brother

2 Thessalonians 3:6-15

We all face the challenges posed by others who behave disorderly. That is, they are busybodies who are unwilling to work. This does not refer to those who are physically or mentally unable to work but to people who refuse to work. The church must recognize the condition and deal with the disorderly brother or sister. As a result, the church must not keep company with them. Rather, the church should shame them into repentance.

> But we command you, brethren, in the name of our Lord Jesus Christ, that you withdraw from every brother who walks disorderly and not according to the tradition which he received from us. For you yourselves know how you ought to follow us, for we were not disorderly among you; nor did we eat anyone's bread free of charge, but worked with labor and toil night and day, that we might not be a burden to any of you, not because we do not have authority, but to make ourselves an example of how you should follow us. For even when we were with you, we commanded you this: If anyone will not work, neither shall he eat. For we hear that there are some who walk among you in a disorderly manner, not working at all, but are busybodies. Now those who are such we command and exhort through our Lord Jesus Christ that they work in quietness and eat their own bread. But *as for* you, brethren, do not grow weary *in* doing good. And if anyone does not obey

our word in this epistle, note that person and do not keep company with him, that he may be ashamed. Yet do not count *him* as an enemy, but admonish him as a brother.
—2 Thessalonians 3:6-16

As we can see, the Apostle and his team gave an example of how to behave when it came to laboring for one's wages. Working for one's keep is normal and expected in the body of Christ and society. Slackers who refuse to work must be singled out and disciplined.

Only once in thirty-five years did a church I pastored need to deal with this challenge. We had a lady who constantly came to the church for help. She always managed to pay back what she borrowed. She did have a debilitating condition. Our Associate Pastor found a job she could easily accomplish. However, she refused to take it on the grounds that it might keep her from receiving disability payments from the state. At this point in her life, she could work. We cut her off from assistance.

The last portion of the admonition in this discipline situation was the "shunning" of such an individual so they may be ashamed. This is one of the few places where someone is to be shamed. Applying this prescription requires tough love.

This prescription applies in church situations. However, the directives here may also apply at work and in community-minded groups. Use discretion. Take care not to injure a party publicly.

2 Thessalonians 3:6-15

The Problem	A believer is behaving in a disorderly manner: not providing for one's needs, a busybody
The Parties Involved	The church and the disorderly brother or sister
The Problem Solver	The church
The Process	1. Recognize the situation 2. Admonish the brother or sister to become orderly 3. Do not keep company with them if they refuse the church's overtures
The Purpose	Repentance and restoration to full fellowship
The Result	The disorderly brother or sister would be shamed into repentance

Figure 9

Points to Ponder

1. Do you know a freeloader or a busybody?

2. How do you handle those who are "disorderly?"

3. Are you overly tenderhearted? If so, you may have difficulty with tough love.

4. Do you tend to be harsh? Beware that you do not simply steamroll anyone whom you perceive to be weak or in your way.

Sexual Immorality in the Church

1 Corinthians 5:1-8

Sexual immorality, a problem from the early annals of Biblical literature and the writings of the ancients, continues to plague us today. This problem does not exist in only one culture or a single ethnic group. This challenge transcends cultures and continents. If one carefully traces the life of King David in ancient Israel, one sees his life as a continuous string of victories even as he faced major challenges. Unfortunately, after his affair with Bathsheba and the murder of Uriah, the Hittite, his life took a decidedly bad turn. The Lord spared his life but did not spare him from challenges within his own family, as his children practiced the same types of behavior. Immorality is no less destructive today!

Sexual promiscuity remains a prominent issue of church discipline. Some years ago, an eighteen-year-old female high school graduate moved in with a forty-year-old man and his fourteen-year-old son. I often wonder how this worked as the young man grew into adulthood. Her home life was poor, which contributed to her attraction to the forty-year-old. In her mind, any place was better than home.

My associate pastor and I visited with her. She stated, "God may strike me dead tomorrow, but I'm not leaving." My associate said, "We need to get two other witnesses" (Matthew 18:15-18). I responded, "This case is not a Matthew 18 situation. This immorality is a 1 Corinthians 5:1-8 situation."

When I read a letter to the church outlining her rebellion, I could not finish reading it. as I became overwhelmed with sadness at her ungodly choices. One of our leaders completed reading it for me. We explained that the church must act. A woman from the back of the auditorium said, "If you discipline this young lady, you will have to discipline half of the church." I did not respond to her comment, but I nearly said, "If that's the case, then yes, we will."

These situations cause much sleeplessness and significant prayer. Difficult? Yes! Painful? Yes! Needed? Absolutely!

The Apostle Paul clearly outlines the process for dealing with sexual immorality in the churches in his first letter to the Corinthians.

It is actually reported that there is sexual immorality among you, and such sexual immorality as is not even named among the Gentiles — that a man has his father's wife! And you are puffed up and have not rather mourned, that he who has done this deed might be taken away from among you. For I indeed, as absent in body but present in spirit, have already judged (as though I were present) him who has so done this deed. In the name of our Lord Jesus Christ, when you are gathered together, along with my spirit, with the power of our Lord Jesus Christ, deliver such a one to Satan for the destruction of the flesh, that his spirit may be saved in the day of the Lord Jesus. Your glorying *is* not good. Do you not know that a little leaven leavens the whole lump? Therefore, purge out the old leaven, that you may be a new lump since you truly are unleavened. For indeed Christ, our Passover, was sacrificed for us. Therefore, let us keep the feast, not with old leaven, nor with the leaven of malice and wickedness, but with the unleavened *bread* of sincerity and truth.—1 Corinthians 5:1-8

Here's the process: First, a case of immorality is identified. The church and the immoral person are involved in the discipline. Once again, the church needs to establish the facts. If repentance takes place, then praise the Lord. The discipline demands no further action. If not, the church must dismiss the offending party from the fellowship. Notice in the above passage that the Apostle did not address the stepmother (apparently, she was not a believer nor a part of the church).

The egregious sin allowed by the Corinthian church was anathema in both Roman and Jewish culture. It appears that neither this individual nor the church shared remorse over this heinous sin.

The passage raises two options related to this individual's temporal and eternal fate. The two options:

- The man experienced premature death, but his soul was saved.
- The man endured significant discipline, repented and was later restored to fellowship (cf. 2 Corinthians 2:5-11), and his soul was, likewise, saved.

Good, godly scholars are divided over the correct interpretation. A. T. Robertson and Mare take the opposite positions on this question from Lowery.[51] Lowery opts for premature physical death, while Robertson and Mare choose bodily discipline and restoration in this life.

---

51   D. K. Lowery, (1985). 1 Corinthians. In J. F. Walvoord & R. B. Zuck (Eds.), The Bible Knowledge Commentary: An Exposition of the Scriptures (Vol. 2, p. 514). Victor Books. "The translation of the Greek word sarkos by the sinful nature suggests the idea that the man's fleshly appetites were to be annulled. However, several factors suggest a different discipline, namely corporeal affliction—with sarkos understood as "body" (as in the NIV margin). (The result, of course, is the same—the man's purification.) First, the latter is the usual meaning of the term when it is juxtaposed with spirit, which signifies the whole man in his inner and external being. Second, the word translated destroyed (olethron) is a strong term, the noun form of which (olethreutou) occurs elsewhere in this letter (10:10) where it is translated "the destroying angel" who killed men. Third, Paul also spoke in this letter about a discipline which leads to death (11:30) with the same end in view—the ultimate preservation of the person (11:32; cf. 1 Tim. 1:20; 1 John 5:16). "So it seems probable that Paul intended this man should be excluded from the fellowship of the congregation, thus physically expressing his exclusion from God's protection which he formerly enjoyed (cf. Job 1:12) and thrusting him out into the arena of the world (1 John 5:19) where Satan would bring about his death. It thus became a painful example of the price of self-centered indifference and a powerful reminder of the demand for holiness in God's temple (1 Cor. 3:17; 6:19)." A.T. Robertson, referring to this text, states, **For the destruction of the flesh** (εἰς ὄλεθρον τῆς σαρκος [eis olethron tēs sarkos]). Both for physical suffering, as in the case of Job (Job 2:6) and for conquest of the fleshly sins, remedial punishment. **That the spirit may be saved** (ἱνα το πνευμα σωθη [hina to pneuma sōthēi]). The ultimate purpose of the expulsion as discipline. Note the use of το

In either case, the eternal state of the believer is settled because of his relationship with Christ. However, those removed from the church body no longer enjoy a hedge of protection provided by the Lord. That's what the Apostle had in mind when he directed the church to "deliver such a one to Satan for the destruction of the flesh."

I have observed both premature death and temporal discipline that led to repentance. The Lord apparently uses both methods, and we do not possess Paul's apostolic authority.

Here is a case where repentance occurred. A man from a church I pastored entered an immoral relationship with a woman. After confronting him, he repented. The church body met with him after our Sunday morning worship service. We invited only the members to remain to deal with this church business. This issue only concerned those who belonged to the fellowship.

As a consequence, this brother experienced restoration and renewed joy in his walk with the Lord Jesus Christ. People in the church took notice, and the church body grew stronger. The

---

πνευμα [*to pneuma*] in contrast with σαρξ [*sarx*] as the seat of personality (cf. 3:15). Paul's motive is not merely vindictive, but the reformation of the offender who is not named here nor in 2 Cor. 2:5-11 if the same man is meant, which is very doubtful. The final salvation of the man in the day of Christ is the goal, and this is to be attained not by condoning his sin." Robertson, A. T. (1933). *Word Pictures in the New Testament* (1 Co 5:5). Broadman Press. https://ref.ly/logosres/LLS:46.50.2?off=2816209. W. Harold Mare, *Expositor's Bible Commentary, Volume 10, Romans Through Galatians* (Grand Rapids, Zondervan, 2011) in loc., takes the view that the discipline was punitive, not fatal. "But, second, the precise punishment intended by Paul is couched in language which the present generation cannot readily understand. The culprit is not only to be excluded from Christian communion, but "to be delivered unto Satan for the destruction of the flesh, that the spirit may be saved." Many meanings have been put upon these words, but after all has been said, the natural and obvious meaning of the words asserts itself. Paul believed that certain sins were more likely to be cured by bodily suffering than by any other agency. Naturally, sins of the flesh belonged to this class. Bodily suffering of some kinds he believed to be the infliction of Satan. Even his own thorn in the flesh he spoke of as a messenger of Satan sent to buffet him. He expected also that the judgment pronounced by himself and the congregation on this offender would be given effect to in God's providence; and accordingly, he bids the congregation hand the man over to this disciplinary suffering, not as a final doom, but as the only likely means of saving his soul. If the offender mentioned in the Second Epistle is the same man, then we have evidence that the discipline was effectual, that the sinner did repent and was overwhelmed with shame and sorrow. Certainly, such an experience of punishment, though not invariably or even commonly effectual, is in itself calculated to penetrate to the very depths of a man's spirit and give him new thoughts about his sin."

man's father is a good friend, and even through the process, our friendship grew. God always honors those who do God's work God's way, difficult as it may seem!

1 Corinthians 5:1-8

The Problem	Immorality in the Church
The Parties Involved	The immoral person and the church
The Problem Solver	The church and the immoral person
The Process	1. Recognize the immorality of a believer in the church
	2. Confront the person
	3. If repentance occurs, then praise the Lord
	4. If repentance fails to take place, deliver the person to Satan for the destruction of the flesh
The Purpose	To cleanse the church from immorality
The Result	The church is cleansed from immorality

Figure 10

Points to Ponder

1. Have you observed this type of church discipline?

2. Did the church handle the challenge well?

3. What outcomes did you observe?

False Teaching and Blasphemous Speech
1 Timothy 1:18-20 and 2 Timothy 2:16-18

In the mid-first century, false teaching and blasphemous speech entered churches. The Apostle Paul did not sit by and watch it happen. He dealt with this major problem. The two passages cited in this section deal with both debilitating issues. They are written not just for the first-century church but also for us. The same problems plague us just as they did nearly 2,000 years ago.

> This charge I commit to you, son Timothy, according to the prophecies previously made concerning you, that by them you may wage the good warfare, having faith and a good conscience, which some having rejected, concerning the faith have suffered shipwreck, of whom are Hymenaeus and Alexander, whom I delivered to Satan that they may learn not to blaspheme. —1 Timothy 1:18-20

> But shun profane *and* idle babblings, for they will increase to more ungodliness. And their message will spread like cancer. Hymenaeus and Philetus are of this sort, who have strayed concerning the truth, saying that the resurrection is already past, and they overthrow the faith of some. —2 Timothy 2:16-18

The problem is that these kinds of individuals promote false teaching and use blasphemous (slanderous) speech. In so doing, they create questions in the minds of believers and cause others to stumble in their faith. These attitudes and actions disrupt the normal flow of church life, harm the body, and cause outsiders to either denigrate the church or avoid it entirely.

These kinds of individuals also affect businesses and companies. Nothing good ever comes from their antics. Chronic complainers and seditious individuals poison relationships, cutting productivity and damaging morale.

How are we to handle these situations? The church body,[52] the slanderers, and the false teachers must be involved in conflict resolution. After all, their tactics impact everyone in the church.

The process includes facing this challenge. The purpose is either repentance or removal from the fellowship. The purpose is to restore health and wholeness to the church and put an end to these deceitful and damaging practices. The ultimate result is once again harmony in the church body.

Here is a personal illustration of the problem of false teaching.

During a leadership meeting at a church where I pastored in the 1980s, the deacons said, "Gordon, we think we have a problem. Edna (not her real name) is leading a Bible study with all of our wives in attendance. She claims that Jesus was not really a man who had human flesh." (One encouraging item is that each deacon and his wife searched the Scriptures on their own and came to the correct conclusions). I immediately knew that we had a problem.

Here are a couple of passages that deal with this heresy.

By this you know the Spirit of God: Every spirit that confesses that Jesus Christ has come in the flesh is of God, and every spirit that does not confess that Jesus Christ has come [in the flesh*] is not of God. And this

---

52   The text does not specifically state that the entire church is involved. However, the pattern in Matthew 18:15-18, 1 Corinthians 5:1-8 and Titus 3:10-11, the church body administers the discipline. After all, these issues impact everyone in the church, not just the leaders.

is the *spirit* of the Antichrist, which you have heard was coming and is now already in the world. —1 John 4:2-3 *The Majority Text includes this phrase.*

For many deceivers have gone out into the world who do not confess Jesus Christ *as* coming in the flesh. This is a deceiver and an antichrist. —2 John 7

Do you see how false teaching can upset believers? We absolutely need to address this issue for the health of the church.

Edna was already in her late sixties or early seventies, so I wanted to treat her with kindness and respect. She also served on the pulpit committee that interviewed me.

When I visited Edna, I made a mistake by going alone. None of the other leaders could or would make the trip with me. I intended to research the situation and ascertain what Edna believed and taught during this preliminary visit. I said, "Edna, I understand that you don't believe that Jesus was really a man." She said, "That is correct."

I came quite well prepared, so I said, "What do you do with 1 Timothy 2:5, 'There is one Mediator between God and men, **the Man** Christ Jesus' (emphasis mine)? How would you respond to that statement?"

Edna said plainly, "Paul made a mistake."

I responded spontaneously, "Houston, we have a problem."

Edna graciously removed herself from the church fellowship. Had she not done so, we would have removed her. Unfortunately, she died a lonely woman a few years later. She never repented of her false teaching. I wept for her.

1 Timothy 1:18-20 ; 2 Timothy 2:16-18	
The Problem	False doctrine and blasphemous speech
The Parties Involved	Teachers of false doctrine and blasphemers, along with the church
The Problem Solver	The leaders and the church seek confession and repentance
The Process	1. Identify and verify the issues 2. Confront the blasphemy and false teaching 3. Seek confession of sin and repentance 4. Deliver the unrepentant to Satan that they may learn not to blaspheme
The Purpose	Restoration to harmony in the body
The Result	1. Restoration 2. Removal from the church if there is no repentance

Figure 11

Discipline for a Sinful Leader

1Timothy 5:19-20

I taught a Doctor of Ministry Cohort at Talbot Seminary, Biola, during the COVID-19 Pandemic. We looked at the issues discussed in this section of the book. One of my students, a church planter from New York City, thanked me for this material. He said, "Gordon, we are dealing with three major conflict issues in our church right now. We are all stressed because we do not know which way to turn." He continued, "We have a leader who constantly lives with sinful behaviors and attitudes. He even flaunts it." Prior to this conversation, I had never addressed 1 Timothy 5:19-20, which speaks to the issue of sinful behavior by a spiritual leader. This passage clearly addresses the problem of persistently sinful behavior in a leader.

We have seen many unfortunate incidents of larger-than-life pastors failing. Some of these failures are due to immorality. However, a growing number of these are due to a failure in leadership style. These types of failures are not limited to large churches. Narcissism and controlling, abusive behavior top the list. I regularly hear from people about their abusive pastor. The sad truth is that people leave their church rather than confronting leadership issues, allowing the sinful behavior to continue.

Here is an example of a church that did confront this form of ungodly behavior. In a small church, a new pastor accused a godly elder of lying. This elder maintained a history of decades of good, godly, humble leadership. This incident was one episode in a long string of abusive behaviors. The church leadership endeavored to work with the pastor but to no avail. He continued to act as God's singular gift to the world and that church. Meaningful conversations about issues did not occur. Eighteen months later, the church dismissed that pastor. He expressed fury with the church but refused to see his failings as a leader. Blinded by his ambition, he did not see how his pride torpedoed his ministry. As someone observed, "Pride is the sinful issue that everyone sees except the one who exhibits it."

Here is a passage that speaks clearly to this issue of a failure of elders (the terms pastor, elder and overseer all refer to the same people in a church leadership structure. See Acts 20:17, 28, 1 Peter 5:1-2).

> Do not receive an accusation against an elder except from two or three witnesses. Those who are sinning rebuke in the **presence** of all, that the rest also may fear (emphasis mine) —1 Timothy 5:19-20

Wise leaders and churches serve themselves well when they proactively deal with sinful leaders. We all sin. This passage speaks to the issue of a pastor/elder/overseer who constantly sins (present active participle in Greek, which implies regular, repeated actions). When churches fail to act, the results are normally disastrous. But when churches do respond to sinful behaviors among the leadership, the ministry has every opportunity to grow and flourish!

1 Timothy 5:19 – 20

The Problem	A church leader is observed continuously practicing sin
The Parties Involved	The leader and two or three witnesses. Ultimately the church
The Problem Solver	The witnesses, church leadership, the sinful leader and ultimately, the church
The Process	1. Two or three witnesses observe a leader's repeated failures 2. The behaviors are reported to the church leadership 3. The issues are confirmed 4. The leader is rebuked before all
The Purpose	1. To address sinful leadership behavior 2. To confirm sinful practices 3. To confront sinful practices 4. To rebuke openly sinful the leader's practices 5. To act as a warning for all that sinful practices will not be tolerated
The Result	1. Restoration 2. Removal from the church if there is no repentance

Figure 12

Dealing with Divisive People

Titus 3:1-11

Here is an account from Pastor Larry Osborne that is repeated in thousands of churches across our land. The issue is the selection of key church leaders. The problem is the silence of the sacrificial lambs who must endure bad leaders. Often, the issue here is the failure of people to break the sound barrier.

> In the front of the room stood an old blackboard filled with names, each a potential nominee for the deacon board. There must have been twenty-five on the list, more than enough to fill the eight slots. Then, just as the meeting was about to close, someone suggested a name. Dutifully, the chairman put it on the board.
>
> Immediately, one of the other staff pastors leaned over to me and whispered, "They've got to be kidding!"
>
> I nodded. All of us on the staff knew what his election would mean: trouble!
>
> He was a man of great personal charisma, an expert at "God talk." But behind the scenes, he was contentious and critical. To make matters worse, he was a disciple and personal friend of one of the most rigid Bible teachers in the nation. Always quick to notice an interpretation or practice that differed from his favorite scholar's, he was apt to see a conspiracy behind any decision he didn't like.
>
> We waited for the senior pastor, the chairman of the board, or someone to speak up, but no one did. Apparently, they figured it wasn't worth the risk of further alienating him

and his friends. Besides that, his name was at the bottom of the list, too far down to have a serious chance of making the final ballot.

But one month later, there the man was, one of the final nominees presented at our annual congregational meeting. His name had worked its way up the list when many of those ahead of him had been unwilling or unable to run for office. Sure enough, he was elected to a three-year term, during which he became a major source of division. Fortunately, his term ended early when he left the church in a huff over a decision he didn't like.[53]

This church was fortunate that he didn't stick it out. Virtually every church I served "enjoyed" such an individual. What does a church do when a situation becomes untenable?

Paul urged Titus to deal with divisive individuals in the congregations he served. "Reject a divisive man after the first and second admonition, knowing that such a person is warped and sinning, being self-condemned" (Titus 3:10-11). The word "reject" demands separation from individuals who intentionally divide the church body.[54] Litfin explains the need to remove these offenders.

Paul's instructions to Titus were direct and specific. He was to give such a person two warnings. If that did not work, he was to have nothing to do with him. The assumption is that a failure to respond to two warnings is a clear sign

53   Larry W. Osborne," Guarding the Gate," Leadership Magazine, https://www.christianitytoday.com/pastors/1990/spring/90l2070.html, accessed December 2, 2023.
54   Bauer, Arndt, and Gingrich, 621, define "reject (Gr. paraitou) as "reject or refuse to do something to someone.... who are younger (than 60 years of age), Titus 3:10, but here perh[aps] the word has the sense dismiss drive out."

that the offender is warped, sinful, and self-condemned. Paul's thought here is similar to the Lord's instructions (Matthew 18:15-18) when He taught that after giving an offender three chances to repent, he is then to be cut off.[55]

This problem, when unchecked, destroys more churches and pastors than any of the other issues we cite. Most people have no appetite for conflict and become paralyzed when facing a church bully or bullies. Our inner being screams for relief, but few are willing to take on these over-dominant individuals in church discipline. Consequently, churches die, and pastors and their families suffer untold agony. Often, the desire for control fuels this behavior. This issue sends many pastors packing. Gene Wood states in his Ninety-Five Percent Theory that "95 percent of all serious problems in the church stem from a power struggle." He continues:

Power struggles … are, in fact, by definition fundamentally irresolvable. The question in a power struggle is, who will lead and who will leave? American culture has contributed to the unwillingness of many church leaders to deal with power struggles. Our government functions with a two-party system. There is always one party in power and a rival party seeking to strip them of this power and place themselves in leadership.[56]

One of my pastor friends invited a controlling antagonist to lunch. As they sat at the table in the middle of a busy restaurant, the pastor said, "This church is not big enough for the two of us,

---

55   A. D. Litfin, Titus. In the Bible Knowledge Commentary ed. John F. Walvoord and Roy B. Zuck (Wheaton: Victor Books, 1983) 2:767.

56   Gene Wood, *Leading Turnaround Churches* (St. Charles: ChurchSmart, 2001), 47..

and I'm not leaving." The opponent stood to his feet in rage and furiously sputtered, "I'm leaving, and I'm taking as many people with me as I possibly can." The pastor rejoined, "Please do!"

A colleague of my friend, Bud Brown, confronted a disruptive member of a troubled church where he served as an intentional interim pastor. The church bully was an influential figure, a member of the Board and a major financial contributor. The pastor met him at a well-traveled coffee shop in town. They sat in the middle of the restaurant, surrounded by the breakfast crowd. (The bully was well-known for being volatile in closed quarters, but he was a prominent businessman in town who would want to protect his reputation). After the coffee was poured, the pastor opened the conversation with, "You've been a serious disruption in the church, and you've tried to stop me at every turn. I need to know when that's going to stop so that I can make plans for your removal if it doesn't." When it was clear that the pastor meant it, the problem stopped after the first warning. The pastors in both accounts kept the circle small, applied the proper biblical text to the situation, and went to the offending party as soon as they knew. That is turnaround leadership, as he employed best practices in dealing with a disruptive bully. They were willing to put it all on the line to halt the bully's corrosive effect on the church.

These truths reflect Proverbs 22:10, "Cast out the scoffer, and contention will leave; Yes, strife and reproach will cease." The peace that follows the departure of a divisive individual is tangible.

My first excursion into the world of major church conflict as a peacemaker occurred in 2003. The trouble revolved around two bullies, Al and Joe (names changed). These two alpha males each tried to lead the congregation in their chosen direction—opposing one another. Everyone knew this tug-of-war existed, but no one would deal with it. Once again, the lambs remained silent. As a result, the church "grew" from 130 to 30 faithful attendees.

I joined a Fresh Start team led by my mentor and friend, Bob Humphry. He was a veteran of many of these wars. After the assessment, we knew where the problems lay. During a Solemn Assembly, we asked each one to confess sins committed against others. One of the bullies, a Moody Bible graduate, pulled a slip of paper from his Scofield Reference Bible. He plainly stated to the other bully, "I've treated you worse than a dog. For that, I am profoundly sorry. He then listed ten ways in which he treated his brother with contempt. I mentally checked off each one in my mind. He pretty well covered the transgressions.

At the conclusion of the successful three-and-one-half-hour Solemn Assembly, we celebrated the Lord's table. During this time, we asked everyone in the room to serve the elements to someone else in the room. When the room grew quiet. I thought perhaps everyone was done. When I looked up, I saw the Scofield bully serving his "enemy." I lost it, weeping tears of joy!

The two bullies admitted and confessed their sins, and we required neither of them to leave. Unfortunately, the church closed a couple of years later because of the extensive collateral damage. My heart still aches for this church of dueling bullies. May their tribe fail to increase!

Years before I served my third congregation, an extremely divisive individual left. Everyone breathed a sigh of relief. A couple of years after we arrived, he and his wife returned to kick the tires of the new pastor to see if he could control me. The day they returned, anxiety immediately returned to the congregation. Their nervousness was palpable. The couple exited the church about a year later after they failed to regain control of the church. Once again, the church breathed a sigh of relief. Their departure was an Alka Seltzer moment! "Plop, plop, fizz, fizz, oh, what. …"

Titus 3:1 – 11	
The Problem	A divisive person disrupts the church
The Parties Involved	The disruptor, the church leadership and the church
The Problem Solver	The leadership, the church and the disruptor
The Process	1. Give two warnings 2. If there is a third incidence of disruption, the member is removed from the church by the church (see also Matt 18:18)
The Purpose	Repentance and restoration. If not, a removal that leads to harmony.
The Result	Restoration in the church body

Figure 13

Stopping Gossip Dead in Its Tracks

Gossip continues to be a bane in society. It ruins lives, destroys relationships, damages reputations and costs immeasurable amounts of human capital. Gossip may be the greatest detriment to effective ministry.

Years ago, R. G. Letourneau, owner of a large earth-moving equipment company, told this story. "We used to have a scraper (an earthmover) known as the Model 'G'. Someone asked one of our salesmen one day what the 'G' stood for. The salesman was pretty quick on the trigger. After thinking for a few seconds, he replied, "Well, I guess the 'G' stands for gossip because, like gossip, this machine moves a lot of dirt and moves it fast!"[57] What an apt description of gossip.

---

57 *Pulpit Helps,* August 1987.

The primary difference between dirt and gossip is that gossip can prove to be deadly!

> A teenage girl attended a very important event with her girlfriend. Both wore long evening gowns. After the party, the girlfriend invited her to spend the night. The girl called her parents and received their approval. The next morning, since she had not brought a change of clothes, she had no choice but to put on the long gown. The girlfriend's father drove her to her home. A neighbor saw her get out of the man's car wearing her long evening gown. So, he put out the rumor that the girl had spent the previous night with a married man. The accusations and misrepresentations that the girl received were so severe that a few weeks later, she put a gun to her head and took her own life.[58]

Proverbs 18:20-21 speaks clearly to this issue of life and death holstered in the tongue.

> A man's stomach shall be satisfied from the fruit of his mouth; *from* the produce of his lips, he shall be filled. Death and life *are* in the power of the tongue, and those who love it will eat its fruit."

What does the text mean when it says, "Those who love it will eat its fruit?" The Bible Knowledge Commentary weighs in on this question.

> A person's words, figuratively called **the fruit of his mouth** (cf. "fruit of his lips," 12:14; 13:2) and **the harvest from his lips**, can benefit himself when his words are

---

58   Larry Moyer, "The Toolbox," (Evantel, February-April 1988).

positive and uplifting. However, one's words (**tongue**) may bring **death** as well as **life**. A witness in a court, for example, can help determine by his words whether a defendant lives or dies. **Those who love it** (the tongue) refers to people who are talkative (cf. 10:19; 18:2; 20:19); they will suffer the consequences (**eat** the **fruit;** cf. 18:20) of what they say.[59]

Therefore, we must guard the tongue, for its use bears great weight and great responsibility.

Here are a few other passages that spell out the dangers of gossip and the tongue.

- The hypocrite with *his* mouth destroys his neighbor, but through knowledge, the righteous will be delivered. Proverbs 11:9.

- He who is devoid of wisdom despises his neighbor, but a man of understanding holds his peace. A talebearer reveals secrets, but he who is of a faithful spirit conceals a matter. Proverbs 11:12-13

- A perverse man sows strife, and a whisperer **separates the best of friends.** (emphasis is mine) Proverbs 16:28

- He who covers a transgression seeks love, but he who repeats a matter separates friends. Proverbs 17:9

- For I fear lest, when I come, I shall not find you such as I wish, and *that* I shall be found by you such as you do not wish; lest *there be* contentions, jealousies, outbursts of wrath, selfish ambitions, backbitings, **whisperings**, conceits, tumults (emphasis mine). 2 Corinthians 12:20

59   Buzzell, S. S., Proverbs. In The Bible Knowledge Commentary, ed. J. F. Walvoord & R. B. Zuck (Wheaton, Victor Books, 1983) 1: 945).

- Wrath *is* cruel, and anger is a torrent, but who *is* able to stand before jealousy? Proverbs 27:4 (Note: Jealousy often fuels gossip!)

- The words of a talebearer *are* like tasty trifles, and they go down into the inmost body. Fervent lips with a wicked heart *are like* earthenware covered with silver dross. He who hates disguises *it* with his lips and lays up deceit within himself; When he speaks kindly, do not believe him, for *there are* seven abominations in his heart; *though his* hatred is covered by deceit, his wickedness will be revealed before the assembly. Proverbs 22:22-26

Note the contrast between those who hold their tongue and those who turn it loose. The potential damage is enormous, even between friends. Eventually, the fruit of gossip will come home to roost. Like a henhouse, your life can become quite messy!

Look over these Proverbs. Mark the ones that apply to you. Ask a close friend or trusted associate if any of these statements fit you. If so, you need to repent and surrender your heart and tongue to the Lord. Otherwise, you will continually damage those near you—family members, church associates, coworkers and friends.

People often wonder who gossips the most: men or women. I know that both sexes indulge in gossip. However, research shows that women use more indirect methods to show their aggression. Men are known to be more violently aggressive than women. Here is a sample from a lengthy article dealing with this issue of indirect aggression, which includes gossip! Here are some brief citations about aggressive behavior in women.

We review the literature on aggression in women with an emphasis on laboratory experimentation and hormonal and brain mechanisms. Women tend to engage in more indirect forms of aggression (e.g., spreading rumors) than other types of aggression. In laboratory studies, women are less aggressive than men, but provocation attenuates this difference. ...

Aggression is a complex social behavior with many causes and manifestations. Over the past several decades, scholars have identified the many forms that aggression can take. Aggression can be physical (e.g., slapping) or verbal (e.g., shouting abuse). It can be direct in nature (e.g., directly retaliating against a co-worker) or indirect with [the] aim of inflicting reputational harm (e.g., spreading rumors about a co-worker behind their back). Aggression can be impulsive, elicited by anger in response to provocation (known as reactive or hostile aggression), or it can be pre-meditated, less emotional, and used as a means to obtain some other end (known as proactive or instrumental aggression). Aggression that is physically extreme is referred to as violence (e.g., aggravated assault, homicide). Despite their apparently different surface characteristics, these in-stantiations of aggression all conform to the scholarly defi-nition of aggression as behavior intended to cause harm to someone who is motivated to avoid that harm (Berkowitz, 1993; Baron and Richardson, 1994; Geen, 2001; Anderson and Bushman, 2002). [60]

---

60   Denson, O'Dean, Blake, and Beames, "Aggression in Women: Behavior, Brain and Hormones," Frontiers in Behavioral Neuroscience," https://www.frontiersin.org/articles/10.3389/fnbeh.2018.00081/full, accessed November 20, 2023. 1-2. The writers agree that much more needs to be done in understanding women's aggression. However, women tend to use less direct modes of aggression—rumors and gossip, while men tend to be more physical.

The writers of this article agree that researchers need to do much more work to help understand women's aggression. However, women tend to use less direct modes of aggression, rumors and gossip than men, while men tend to be more aggressive physically.

Gossip affects both men and women. Regardless of the perpetrators of gossip and rumor-mongering, we must make a concerted effort to stop the damage gossip causes.

I would like us to consider one further Proverb that speaks to the need to stop gossip.

> Where *there is* no wood, the fire goes out, and where *there is* no talebearer, strife ceases. *As* charcoal *is* to burning coals and wood to fire, so *is* a contentious man to kindle strife. The words of a talebearer *are* like tasty trifles, and they go down into the inmost body. —Proverbs 26:20-22

Notice that the "fire" goes out when we no longer stack gossip logs on the flames. In our interpersonal relationships, we must hold up a giant red stop sign when we hear gossip. We cannot allow these rumors to sink into our souls, nor can we be a part of the feeding frenzy that occurs when gossip goes unmitigated. Here are four steps we should take when gossip happens in our presence.

1. Be Direct. Identify the source of gossip by name.
2. Seek the facts. Make sure truth, not innuendo, is shared.
3. Promise to quote them by name. This may stop gossipers in their tracks.
4. Be Direct. Tell those bearing gossip to stop. Inform them that you don't want any part of their rumor mill. This may cost you, but this step may help staunch the bleeding caused by gossip.

One of the great difficulties today with the use of technology and social media is that gossip now travels at blinding speed via social media. Once you ring the bell, you can't unring it!

Here is an account from yesteryear that sheds light on the impact of gossip today. The source of the quote is unknown.

A young monk spread a false rumor around town to all who would listen. His Abbott discovered his transgression. The young man felt terrible. As penance, the Abbott gave him a task. "Go and place a feather on the stoop of every home where you spread this malicious rumor."

The young monk thought, "That's simple enough. I can do that."

So, with a light heart, he proceeded through town and placed a feather on the stoop of every home where he gossiped. He returned to the Abbott and said, "I've completed my penance." The Abbott said, "Not quite! Now return and pick up every feather you placed and bring them back to me."

The young monk said, "That's impossible. By now, the wind has scattered them all over the community. I will never be able to retrieve them all."

"Yes," said the Abbott. "Neither can you ever retrieve the lies you spread. For now, they are scattered all over the community." —Source unknown

Once you ring the bell, you cannot unring it. Social media is a killer (literally). We must be careful and teach our young people and adults alike to be cautious when using social media, for it can destroy lives—at the speed of light.

Here is a rather humorous account about a fellow who stopped a church gossip and a church bully cold! My brother and fellow pastor, J. L. Penfold, shared this story with me!

Mildred, the church gossip and self-appointed monitor of the church's morals, kept sticking her nose into other people's business. Several members did not approve of her extracurricular activities but feared her enough to maintain their silence. She made a mistake, however, when she accused Frank, a new member, of being an alcoholic after she saw his old pickup parked in front of the town's only bar one afternoon.

She emphatically told Frank (and several others within earshot) that everyone seeing it there WOULD KNOW WHAT HE WAS DOING!

Frank, a man of few words, stared at her for a moment and just turned and walked away. He didn't explain, defend, or deny. He said nothing.

Later that evening, Frank quietly parked his pickup in front of Mildred's house, locked the door, walked home, and left it there all night. (You gotta love Frank!)

Points to Ponder

1. Are you one who enjoys gossip? If so, what steps must you take to stop your sinful practice? Repent? Have you asked the Lord to transform you in this arena (Romans 12:1-2)?

2. How do you respond when others gossip with you? Do you practice the steps outlined in this section? This requires you to be strong in your faith!

3. Have you been the object of hurtful gossip?

4. How did this make you feel? How should this impact your own actions?

5. How did you respond?

6. How should you respond in the future?

CHAPTER 12

CHURCH AND CLERGY KILLERS

Some years ago, while passing through Coeur d'Alene, Idaho, I received a call from a pastor in the Lower Arkansas Valley of Colorado, near Las Animas, where I served for fourteen years. He painted an extremely disturbing picture of his situation.

At that time, he suffered from a debilitating disease that waylaid him for several months. While recuperating, a group of people who moved into the church he pastored attempted to oust him from his position. One of his elders, who formerly attended the church I pastored in Las Animas, gave him my number.

It turns out that this group left a once-thriving church, possibly the healthiest church in Southeastern Colorado, to move to this fellowship. They destroyed the pastor in their previous church and deeply damaged the church body before their exit—leaving only an empty shell of the church's former prominence. Now, they focused their destructive crosshairs on this godly pastor and the church fellowship. Fortunately, this church had a strong group of leaders who resisted the black overtures of this satan-influenced coalition. The group left and moved to another church in La Junta. A few months later, this 80-year-old once-thriving fellowship in La Junta shuttered its doors. These diabolical folks placed another notch on their sadistic six-shooters.

We call these types of people Church Killers and Clergy Killers. These folks are like bullies on steroids. Their speech, always couched in churchy language and spiritual jargon, camouflages their desire to destroy ministries and church leaders. Unfortunately, these individuals are deadly, lurking assassins intent on destruction at any cost.

These destroyers exist in every tier of society, not just in the church. They poison relationships and produce toxic environments wherever they touch people. Like cancer, these folks must be excised from your organization, or they will destroy it.

My ministry as Executive Director of Fresh Start Ministry Network often leads me past the carnage of such individuals. How do these demons of hell operate? Dennis Maynard wrote a trilogy dealing with attacks on clergy based on twenty-five case studies of churches attacking their shepherds. The following chart comes from his book. The chart is mine, but the concept belongs to Maynard. [61] It graphically shows how opposition grows from the "facts" to a pastor's or leader's removal. Facts develop into opinions, opinions into innuendo, innuendo grows into accusation, and accusation eventually leads to a leader's dismissal.

61   Dennis R. Maynard, When Sheep Attack (n.p. Booksurge Publishers, 2010), 47-48.

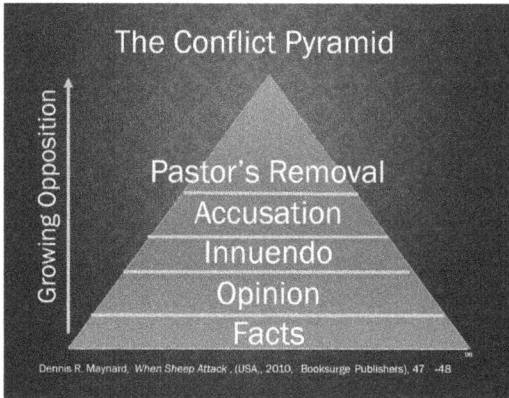

Figure 14
Figure 3. The Conflict Pyramid

I have seen this type of character assassination, and I'll bet you have, too. It's ugly and distasteful. Gossip plays a major role in these diabolical movements, whether in the church, a business or a civic organization.

You absolutely cannot permit these kinds of destroyers in your church or organization. If you allow these behaviors to get a toehold, you must beat it back into the unholy sea from whence it arose. Gossip is inevitable, but you need not tolerate it. Destruction lies on the tip of the tongue. They may begin sowing discord by complaining about the pastor's preaching or the direction of the church. They may call into question the decisions made by godly leaders and may begin to plant seeds of doubt throughout the church or civic group. Eventually, they will violently oppose appointed leaders, resulting in their termination.

At the first sign of trouble, act decisively. As my friend Thom Pratt says, "Run to the sound of conflict!" Peace made in private is better than trying to put out a public firestorm!

PART 5

Your Personality and Mending Fences

CHAPTER 13

YOUR PERSONALITY AND MENDING FENCES

Your personality profile is a major (and often overlooked) element of successful conflict resolution. How do you handle opposition to your plans when you're under stress? A number of tools can be successfully used to understand your responses to conflict better. I already mentioned "Conflict Style Assessment" from NextStep Resources. The DISC Profile will help you know how you behave and how you see the world.

The Taylor-Johnson Temperament Analysis®(T-JTA®) is a widely used personality assessment for individual, pre-marital, marital and family counseling. The T-JTA measures 18 dimensions of personality (9 bipolar traits) that are important in individual adjustment and interpersonal relationships.[62] The Tailor-Johnson Temperament Analysis also points out significant issues that impact your mental and emotional health.

The most effective tool I have found is The Birkman Method®. The Birkman is a positive psychological tool, not designed to test for mental health. It is designed to help individuals and groups

---

62   From the Taylor-Johnson website, tjta.com.

magnify their interpersonal relationships and productivity. Like many other assessments, this tool will help you understand how you show up and how others perceive you, but it adds two other dimensions not found in any other profile.

- The Birkman Method identifies ten Birkman Interests that are derived from responses to the occupational questions on the Birkman questionnaire. The Birkman Interests compare your interest in broad areas of activity with the level of interest most other people have.

- Usual Behavior represents our ideal self and how we think we contribute to our community.

- Needs (or expectations) data represents the Social Perception of the respondent, how they anticipate others will act in a common situation. When we are in the midst of situations that match our Needs, life feels normal, and we remain at our best.

- Stress Behaviors are our reactions to situations that are not comfortable to us, and when things happen that we don't expect.[63]

The Birkman helps us understand how we operate and how we will most likely interact with others. Stress behaviors occur when people fail to meet an individual's "unseen" needs.or expectations. Stress behaviors are never positive and can damage relationships. A great deal of conflict can occur when people do not understand those needs. By understanding our hard wiring, we can more effectively interact with others in challenging

---

63   Birkman International, "Birkman Signature Certification Training Manual—Version 3.3," (Houston, Texas, January 2020) 18, 42, 48, 52.

situations. Self-awareness and awareness of others are vital in conflict management! How much conflict could be avoided if we better perceived others and our environment?

If you would like more information on using the Birkman Method, contact me or one of our associates at Advanced Pastoral Network (https://www.advancedpastoralnetwork.com/).

PART 6

The Necessity of Forgiveness

CHAPTER 14

THE NECESSITY OF FORGIVENESS

Bitterness is like drinking poison and waiting for the other person to die.[64]

We have spent a great deal of time exploring the causes and effects of conflict. We now move into the arena of forgiveness. This section is the culmination and most important piece needed for mending fences. If we handle the causes of conflict but do not respond well with forgiveness, then these processes fall far short of their intended purposes. Forgiveness is **the key** to personal health and wholeness for unity in the Body of Christ, the family and the marketplace.

Dr. Archibald Hart defines forgiveness as "giving up my right to hurt you for hurting me."[65] When we fail to forgive, we only perpetuate our own hurt. Nelson Mandela provided sage wisdom as he was released from prison in South Africa in 1990 after 27 years of incarceration for opposition to apartheid.

---

64   This saying is attributed to Joanna Weaver, Having a Mary Heart in a Martha World. https://www.goodreads.com/quotes/224869-bitterness-is-like-drinking-poison-and-waiting-for-the-other. Accessed December 5, 2023.

65   James Dobson quoting Archibald Hard in "The Only Cure for Bitterness, Dobson's Bulletin, May 1999.

As I walked out that door toward the gate that would lead to my freedom, I knew if I did not leave all the anger, hatred and bitterness behind, I would still be in prison.[66]

I worked with a deeply divided church in 2007. The church split 1/3 to 2/3 over the pastor, with a third supporting his ministry. An interim pastor aided in putting the congregation back together again. Unfortunately, some of the deep-seated issues were never resolved. The congregation coexisted, but they weren't really together. Five years later, I helped with a church assessment. As we interviewed a large percentage of the congregation, we discovered continuing resentment in a number of members but seething bitterness in one.

Apparently, this person sided with the pastor, who resigned under less-than-wonderful conditions. As is the case in every conflict, truth and falsehoods abounded on both sides of the controversy. This lady and one of the deacons found themselves caught up in an explosive argument. The deacon lost his temper, raised his voice and deeply hurt this woman (not physically). Later, the deacon came to her on his own, confessed his sinful actions, apologized and sought forgiveness. Deacon "Frank" freely admitted his sinful outburst to us. He did his part. Unfortunately, the woman never forgave him.

As we visited with her, I said, "Deacon Frank did what the Scriptures required of him. He knew he was out of line. He humbled himself, came to you, freely confessed his sin and sought your forgiveness. Now, it is your responsibility to forgive him."

---

66   https://search.brave.com/search?q=nelson+mandela+on+bitterness&source=desktop Accessed 5/4/2024.

I'll never forget her response. "I can never forgive him. He was out of line, and I WILL NEVER FORGIVE HIM." Her unforgiveness now became her sin!

I was shocked by her disclosure. Think about the three illustrations used above. This woman drank the poison, would not give up her right to hurt him, and dwelt in a prison of her own making. That's the fruit of unforgiveness.

Lewis Smedes said it this way, "To forgive is to set a prisoner free and discover that the prisoner was you."[67]

Does the Word of God say anything about forgiveness? Plenty! Let's look at one passage that throws the spotlight of heaven on this subject: Matthew 18:15-35. Forgiveness is central to this text. Jesus addressed this issue of pride in Matthew 18:1 when the disciples asked him who the greatest was. The disciples even debated this subject in the Upper Room on the night of Christ's betrayal. If they struggled with pride, we should not be surprised that we do the same.

Matthew 18:15-18 is already familiar to us as we looked at it in detail in Part 4. However, we will expand the discussion here. We will look at The Process of Discipline, How Much is Too Much Forgiveness, The Necessity of Forgiveness, and Divine Examples of Forgiveness.

- **The Process of Reconciliation**
- **How Much Forgiveness is Too Much Forgiveness?**
- **The Necessity of Forgiveness**
- **Divine Examples of Forgiveness**

---

67   Lewis Smedes, https://www.brainyquote.com/quotes/lewis_b_smedes_135524 Accessed 8/30/2024.

The Process of Reconciliation

As we discussed in Section 5, Matthew 18:15-18 contains directions and prescriptions for handling issues of one believer who sins against another believer. This is but a fraction of the total passage that looks not only at the issue of sin against a fellow believer but at the entire sphere of forgiveness.

In Section 4, we saw that the process of seeking reconciliation begins by keeping the circle small. The only two people who are privy to the issue are the two who need to know. If reconciliation fails to take place, the circle expands to include two or three reliable witnesses. Should reconciliation fail during this second step, the circle expands greatly as the entire church body is included in the reconciliation process. Note the need to involve the whole congregation in this essential step.

Reconciliation may occur, and we praise the Lord when that occurs. Forgiveness may or may not occur, as we saw in the account of the woman and Deacon Frank.

Handling these cases of intentional sin against another believer bears great weight, not only on earth but also in heaven. We see that the church's action and heaven's acclamation are in accordance with one another.

> Assuredly, I say to you, whatever you bind on earth will be bound in heaven, and whatever you loose on earth will be loosed in heaven. —Matthew 15:18

Young's Literal Translation reads this way:

Verily, I say to you, Whatever things ye may bind upon the earth shall be having been bound in the heavens, and whatever things ye may loose on the earth shall be having been loosed in the heavens.

God says our work in reconciliation reflects His position in heaven! How does this work? The text needs to be clarified. Let these thoughts swirl around in your mind. The Lord takes reconciliation seriously. When we engage in the reconciliation process, the work of the Trinity becomes our work! We must carefully and prayerfully engage in this task.

Pentecost declares, "Unity is a prerequisite to answered prayer."[68] The thought of discipline flows naturally into the need to seek the face of God in prayer. Robertson adds:

Shall agree (Greek—συμφωνησωσιν [*sumphōnēsōsin*]). Our word "symphony" is this very root. It is no longer looked at as a concord of voices, a chorus in harmony, though that would be very appropriate in a church meeting rather than the rasping discord sometimes heard even between two brethren or sisters.[69]

This is a similar refrain to 1 Peter 3:7, where the Lord enjoins husbands to respect their wives lest their prayers be hindered. As Robertson states, "the rasping discord" does not land favorably on the ears of heaven! No wonder so many marriages, churches and groups demonstrate great ineffectiveness. These

---

68   J. Dwight Pentecost, The Words and Works of Jesus Christ: A Study of the Life of Christ (Grand Rapids, Zondervan, 1981), 268.

69   Robertson, A. T. (1933). Word Pictures in the New Testament (Mt 18:19). Broadman Press. https://ref.ly/logosres/LLS:46.50.2?off=313259.

units, operating with their strength, remain weak. Like leeches, unresolved conflict and unforgiveness suck the life blood out of all who indulge.

How Much Forgiveness is Too Much Forgiveness?

The question arose in Peter's mind, "How forgiving must I be?" Dwight Pentecost speaks cogently on this issue.

> The Pharisees taught that righteousness demanded that a person be forgiven twice. If a person wanted to prove himself magnanimous, he forgave three times, but such forgiveness was the limit of the righteousness of the Pharisees. Peter far exceeded the demands of the righteousness of the Pharisees when he suggested that the limit of forgiveness was seven times. Christ taught that the righteousness demanded one to exceed the righteousness of the Pharisees or even the standard that Peter was setting for himself. Jesus said to forgive seventy-seven times [can be translated seventy times seven]. To the Jewish mind, this means times without number[70].

To illustrate this principle of limitless forgiveness on our part, the Lord Jesus shared a parable that describes the necessity of forgiveness.

The Necessity of Forgiveness

The Parable on Forgiveness.

> Then Peter came to Him and said, "Lord, how often shall my brother sin against me, and I forgive him? Up to seven times?"

---

70 Pentecost, 269.

Jesus said to him, "I do not say to you, up to seven times, but up to seventy times seven. Therefore, the kingdom of heaven is like a certain king who wanted to settle accounts with his servants. And when he had begun to settle accounts, one was brought to him who owed him ten thousand talents. But as he was not able to pay, his master commanded that he be sold with his wife and children and all that he had, and that payment be made. The servant therefore fell down before him, saying, 'Master, have patience with me, and I will pay you all.' Then the master of that servant was moved with compassion, released him, and forgave him the debt.

But that servant went out and found one of his fellow servants who owed him a hundred denarii; and he laid hands on him and took him by the throat, saying, 'Pay me what you owe!' So his fellow servant fell down at his feet and begged him, saying, 'Have patience with me, and I will pay you all.' And he would not but went and threw him into prison till he should pay the debt. So when his fellow servants saw what had been done, they were very grieved and came and told their master all that had been done. Then his master, after he had called him, said to him, 'You wicked servant! I forgave you all that debt because you begged me. Should you not also have had compassion on your fellow servant, just as I had pity on you?' And his master was angry and delivered him to the torturers until he should pay all that was due to him." —Matthew 18:21-34

We must note several things in this parable. First, the Lord focuses on two debtors. The first one owed an unpayable debt to the master—10,000 talents. His fellow slave owed him 100 denarii. Here is the financial breakdown. "A talent was, probably, gold that weighed between 58 and 80 pounds.[71] The price of gold fluctuates widely. On December 9, 2023, gold was about $2,002 per ounce, with 12 troy ounces per pound. Thus, at today's value, one talent of gold (58 pounds) would be worth $1,393,392. Add 5-zeros to that for 10,000 talents. Get the picture! He owed more than he could ever pay on a servant's salary! Such is the state of our standing before God. We owe a debt we can never pay. Only Christ could cover such a debt with his death for us!

However, what others do to us is a pittance compared to the debt we owe to Christ. "A hundred denarii (vs. 28) represented a hundred day's wages for a foot soldier or common laborer."[72] Let's do the math. The first debtor owed an incredible $139,339,200,000—the second owed about 100 days' wages—roughly a third of a year's salary. The first servant owed an insurmountable debt, a debt he could never pay. The second debt was doable.

Here's how we should respond to those who offend us. If God's mercy can forgive us a debt we could never pay, then we should be able to forgive those who injure us. What they owe us is nothing in comparison to what we owe the Lord.

Robert Murray M'Cheney penned these words in the third stanza of a poem he wrote in 1837.

> When I stand before the throne,
> Dressed in beauty not my own,
> When I see Thee as Thou art,
> Love Thee with unsinning heart;
> Then, Lord, shall I fully know,
> Not till then, how much I owe.[73]

71   Louis A. Barbieri, Jr., Matthew. In The Bible Knowledge Commentary ed. J. F. Walvoord & R. B. Zuck (Wheaton, Victor Books, 1983), 2: 62.

72   D. A. Carson, "Matthew" in The Expositor's Bible Commentary, ed Frank E. Gaebelein, (Grand Rapids, Zondervan, 1976), 8: Matthew 16:28.

73   Robert Murray M'Chenye, 1837, https://www.mcheyne.info/i-am-a-debtor/

It is easy to judge others by their faults. We need to remind ourselves that our debt before the Lord is 60,000,000 days' wages. Anything anyone can do to us is a pittance compared to what we owe!

In verses 34-35, the Lord addresses the final point of the parable.

> And his master was angry and delivered him to the torturers until he should pay all that was due to him. So My heavenly Father also will do to you if each of you, from his heart, does not forgive his brother his trespasses.

Harsh? Absolutely. Does this mean that a person who does not forgive cannot be saved? Absolutely not! What it does mean is that those who fail to forgive offenses against them will suffer at the hands of torturers. Again, the great Greek scholar A. T. Robertson sheds enormous light on this subject.

Matthew 18:34
The tormentors (Greek, τοις βασανισταις [tois basanistais]). Not to prison simply, but to terrible punishment. The papyri give various instances of the verb βασανιζω [basanizō], to torture, used of slaves and others. "Livy (ii. 23) pictures an old centurion complaining that he was taken by his creditor, not into servitude, but to a workhouse and torture, and showing his back scarred with fresh wounds" (Vincent). Till he should pay all. Just as in verse 30, his very words. But this is not purgatorial but punitive, for he could never pay back that vast debt.

Matthew 18:35
From your hearts (Greek, ἀπο των καρδιων ὑμων [apo tōn kardiōn hūmōn]). No sham or lip pardon, and as often

as needed. This is Christ's full reply to Peter's question in 18:21. This parable of the unmerciful servant is surely needed today.[74]

Ray Stedman, former pastor of Peninsula Bible Church in Palo Alto, CA, describes what happens to people who do not forgive, who hold on to grudges, and who want to get even.

This is a marvelously expressive phrase to describe what happens to us when we do not forgive another. It is an accurate description of gnawing resentment and bitterness, the awful gall of hate or envy. It is a terrible feeling. We cannot get away from it. We feel strongly this separation from another, and every time we think of them, we feel within the acid of resentment and hate eating away at our peace and calmness. This is the torturing that the Lord says will take place.[75]

How do we capture the big idea for this portion of the Word of God? Simple.

**Vertical forgiveness demands horizontal forgiveness.[76]
Horizontal forgiveness produces freedom.**

What happens to you when you think of someone who sinned against you, who damaged your psyche or who insulted you?

74   Robertson, A. T. (1933). Word Pictures in the New Testament (Mt 18:34–35). Broadman Press. https://ref.ly/logosres/LLS:46.50.2?off=318772.

75   Ray C. Stedman, "Breaking the Resentment Barrier," (Sermon delivered to Peninsula Bible Church, Palo Alto, CA, Treasurers of the Parable series, message 11, July 13, 1969, 6. As quoted by Charles R. Swindoll in Improving Your Serve (Waco, Texas, Word, Incorporated, 1981) 66-67

76   Charles Swindoll, Improving Your Serve: The Art of Unselfish Living (Waco, Word Books, 1981) 65. The concept of "vertical and horizontal forgiveness" is found in this volume, though not expressed exactly as I suggest.

What happens when you see that person at the grocery store or in a social setting? Do thoughts of revenge boil up inside you? If this happens, you've not forgiven them.

When you are trying to go to sleep, and their actions cross your mind, do you lie awake thinking of ways you can get even? Do you pray that the Lord would take them out? These things have happened to me. I'm sure they happen to you as well.

What are some of the torturers? Insomnia. Back Trouble. Bitterness. Alcoholism. Restlessness. Anxiety. Ulcers. Anger. Fear. I faced most of them. These torturers are not pleasant as they exact the toll of unforgiveness on my life and you!

In my second D.Min. cohort gathering at Biola in 2008, I attended a church plant. The pastor's message focused on forgiveness and moving on from your pain. At the end of the service, he invited those present to write down on a 3x5 card the names of people who had offended us. We were asked to bring up the names of those who injured us and run the 3x5 cards through the shredders that had been set up at the front of the worship area. I had recently left a church with lots of pain. Writing down the names of those individuals on those cards and asking the Lord to help me forgive went a long way toward the kind of forgiveness I needed to exhibit inwardly.

Today, when I think about some of the injustices, I still see red. I have to stop and say, "Lord, please give me the strength to forgive these people. I know I offended you more deeply than these individuals ever could offend me. Give me the grace to forgive them just as you have forgiven me." With that comes freedom!

Corrie ten Boom suffered through the almost unspeakable horrors of World War II. She and her family helped Jewish people escape the Nazis through Holland. She and her sister ended up at Ravensbrück, a concentration camp in Germany. Her sister died there. She never saw the rest of her family again. She writes about what it was like to see one of the SS troops who tormented the prisoners when he showed up at a church service in Munich after the end of the war. The description of her wild emotions certainly feels familiar.

It was in a church service in Munich that I saw him, the former S.S. man who had stood guard at the shower room door in the processing center at Ravensbruck. He was the first of our actual jailers that I had seen since that time. And suddenly, it was all there—the roomful of mocking men, the heaps of clothing, Betsie's pain-blanched face.

He came up to me as the church was emptying, beaming and bowing, "How grateful I am for your message, Fraulein," he said. "To think that, as you say, he has washed my sins away!"

His hand was thrust out to shake mine. And I, who had preached so often to the people in Bloemendall about the need to forgive, kept my hand at my side.

Even as the angry, vengeful thoughts boiled through me, I saw the sin of them. Jesus Christ had died for this man; was I going to ask for more? "Lord Jesus," I prayed, "forgive me and help me to forgive him."

I tried to smile. I struggled to raise my hand. I could not. I felt nothing, not the slightest spark of warmth or charity. And so, again, I breathed a silent prayer. "Jesus, I cannot forgive him. Give me Your forgiveness."

As I took his hand, the most incredible thing happened. From my shoulder along my arm and through my hand, a current seemed to pass from me to him, while into my heart sprang a love for this stranger that almost overwhelmed.[77]

Corrie Ten Boom discovered that she could not forgive or love her enemy on her own. She could only forgive and love through the power of Christ.

Please let the power of the passage soak into your parched soul. Do not give the torturers any more quarter. Be set free through the forgiveness Christ Jesus provides for us.

You might ask, "Why pursue the remedies of Scripture?" Harmony in the body is at stake. We can confront sinful practices, and we should. However, even if the remedy is found, we must be willing to forgive. Reconciliation without forgiveness will still leave us in debt! Exacting a pound of flesh will never satisfy our souls. Only forgiveness will accomplish that. Consider the following illustration of our need to forgive others.

Several years back, five ladies contacted me about a rhubarb that divided their group. One lady let an issue slip that violated the HIPAA requirements at a local hospital. The four were deeply incensed by her lack of discretion. The resulting mess caused a great deal of anger. One of the ladies had the presence of mind to ask if I could help. I asked all five to spend thirty days of preparation. During those days, I required each of them to read a selected scripture passage each day and then do a short Bible study that required them to ask themselves tough questions about the role they played in the firestorm.

---

77   Corrie ten Boom, The Hiding Place (New York: Bantam, 1974), 238.

We met at the conclusion of the thirty days for a Solemn Assembly that lasted about two and a half hours. We began with more scripture reading, prayer and a season of confession. Each one had to own their own part of the problem. The lady who violated the HIPAA policy spoke first. She readily owned her part of the problem. She asked for forgiveness from God and her friends.

One by one, each one owned her part of the conflict. As our session wound down, one of the ladies pointed an accusing finger at the HIPAA violator and said, "But you are guilty." I stopped her dead in her tracks and said, "We've already covered that. We are done with this issue. We must now move on to reconciliation and forgiveness."

Several others tried to resurrect the transgression. Each time I reminded them of the same truth. "It's time to place this behind you." All too often, we want to act as judge and jury, but we exclude the grace of forgiveness.

The question? "How much forgiveness is too much?" The wages of 60,000,000 days or 100 days' wages?

This scenario is all too familiar. We can work through the biblical processes of reconciliation, but if we continue to harbor bitterness and resentment, we are still bound.

How long will you demand repayment? How often will you dredge up the past and relive your hurt or the hurt of others? How often will a cold shoulder betray the unforgiveness in your soul toward someone who injured you? We need to receive vertical forgiveness from God and extend horizontal forgiveness to those who wrong us. Only then can we be truly free!

Points to Ponder

1. Write down past issues that bobbed to the surface as you read this section.

2. Are you still hanging on to them?

3. Do you need to break the sound barrier before you break down?

4. Like Corrie ten Boom, do you need to ask the Lord for the forgiveness you need to extend to others or forgiveness you must own for yourself? We are not strong enough to do this on our own.

5. Allow the Lord to set you free from the prison you built for yourself.

Divine Examples of Forgiveness

Christ Himself embodies the greatest example of forgiveness. From the cross, He cried out, "Father, forgive them, for they do not know what they do" (Luke 23:34). Were the chief priests, Pilate, the Romans, and the crowds not guilty of sin? Of course, they were. What about the soldiers? Why did the soldiers torment Christ? There are at least three reasons.

1. They were ordered to do so.
2. They loved to inflict pain, suffering and death.
3. It was ordained of God.   Acts 2:23

These greedy, murderous soldiers deserve no quarter. Neither did the bigoted, narrow-minded Pharisees and Sadducees. Nor did Pilate, who bowed spinelessly to the will of the people. What about Herod Antipas? He carried on the long tradition of seeking his own benefit. Nevertheless, Jesus forgave them. His shoes are huge shoes to fill. In our strength—impossible! In the power of the Holy Spirit—possible!

Even the High Priest became a prophet, not knowing his words were on target!

> And one of them, Caiaphas, being high priest that year, said to them, "You know nothing at all, nor do you consider that it is expedient for us that one man should die for the people, and not that the whole nation should perish." Now, this he did not say on his own *authority*, but being high priest that year, he prophesied that Jesus would die for the nation, and not for that nation only, but also that He would gather together in one the children of God who were scattered abroad. —John 11:29-52

This murderous rabble accomplished the greatest deliverance ever conceived in the heart of God or men. In the midst of the hatred and passion to inflict pain, Christ forgave them!

Stephen followed the Lord's example as he was stoned for defending the faith.

> And as they stoned Stephen as he was calling on *God* and saying, "Lord Jesus, receive my spirit." Then he knelt down and cried out with a loud voice, "Lord, do not charge them with this sin." —Acts 7:59-60

The Lord exhorts us in Ephesians 4:32, "Be kind to one another, tenderhearted, forgiving one another, even as God in Christ forgave you."

I came across this account many years ago in *Leadership Magazine*. This incident powerfully reminds us of the need for vertical forgiveness, which leads to horizontal forgiveness, and horizontal forgiveness produces freedom. This account of forgiveness is overwhelming. I ask myself, "Under similar circumstances, could I do the same?" Not in my strength, for certain.

> In an emotionally charged courtroom, a South African woman stood listening to white police officers acknowledge their atrocities.
>
> Officer van de Broek acknowledged that, along with others, he had shot her 18-year-old son at point-blank range. He and the others partied while they burned the son's body, turning it over and over on the fire until it was reduced to ashes.
>
> Eight years later, van de Broek and others returned to seize her husband. She was forced to watch her husband, bound on a woodpile, as they poured gasoline over his body and ignited the flames that consumed his body. The last words she heard her husband say were, "Forgive them."
>
> Now, van de Broek awaited judgment. South Africa's Truth and Reconciliation Commission asked the woman what she wanted.
>
> "I want three things," she said calmly. "I want Mr. van de Broek to take me to the place where they burned my husband's body. I would like to gather up the dust and give him a decent burial.

Second, Mr. van de Broek took all my family away from me, and I still have a lot of love to give. Twice a month, I would like for him to come to the ghetto and spend a day with me so I can be a mother to him.

Third, I would like Mr. van de Broek to know that he is forgiven by God and that I forgive him, too. I would like to embrace him so he can know my forgiveness is real."

As the elderly woman was led across the courtroom, van de Broek fainted, overwhelmed. Someone began singing "Amazing Grace." Gradually, everyone joined in.[78]

I hope you are journeying toward the freedom forgiveness engenders. I know I still have many issues to deal with as I grow in the grace and knowledge of our Lord Jesus Christ.

Points to Ponder

1. The process of outward reconciliation may be complete, but the process of forgiveness must likewise be complete.

2. One may "settle" in the church, but one must also settle in the heart. Has forgiveness settled in your heart, or does bitterness still reign?

---

78   *Leadership,* Spring, 2001 (Leadership is no longer in print. No other publishing information could be found)

Remember:
Vertical forgiveness between you and God
demands horizontal forgiveness between you and others.
Horizontal forgiveness produces FREEDOM.

I want to leave you with one final quote.

Forgiveness is the fragrance that the violet leaves
on the heel of the one who crushed it.[79]

Are you exuding the aroma of heaven, or are you full of the putrid stench of the unforgiving and unforgiven? Where do you struggle?

---

79   Attributed to Mark Twain and a host of others. https://quoteinvestigator.com/2013/09/30/
violet-forgive/. This reference includes the following: An 1812 book by Reverend Charles Colton
discussed forgiveness and employed the same metaphor while citing the words of Sir William Jones
in a footnote. Colton presented a "sandal tree" as an example of a plant that had been "wronged" but
reacted with "forgiveness" and "kindness":
   The falling Sandal-Tree sheds fragrance round,
   Perfumes the axe that fells it to the ground;
   Some through their tortured trunks, a balm supply,
   And to give life to their destroyer—die.

PART 7

Next Steps

CHAPTER 15

NEXT STEPS

Here is a summary to remind us of those needy areas in our lives where we lack peace, fail in interpersonal relationships and deal with difficult people.

- **Lacking Peace with God?**
- **Peace with Our Families**
- **Flashpoints of Conflict that Impact You**
- **Break the Sound Barrier**
- **The Objective and Keys to Peacemaking**
- **Stubborn People Who Refuse to Make Peace**
- **In a Firestorm of Conflict**

Lacking Peace with God?

Do you need to find Peace with God through the God of Peace? In this case, you must recognize that your sin separates you from God. Place your faith in the Lord Jesus Christ as your Savior and Sin-bearer.

Here is the biblical summary of the Gospel. It contains four elements as outlined in 1 Corinthians 15:1-7.

Moreover, brethren, I declare to you the **gospel [good news]** which I preached to you, which also you received and in which you stand, by which also you are saved, if you hold fast that word which I preached to you—unless you believed in vain.

For I delivered to you first of all that which I also received: that **Christ died** for our sins according to the Scriptures, and that **He was buried**, and that **He rose again the third day** according to the Scriptures, and that **He was seen** by Cephas, then by the twelve. After that, He was seen by over five hundred brethren at once, of whom the greater part remain to the present, but some have fallen asleep. After that, He was seen by James, then by all the apostles. Then, last of all, He was seen by me also, as by one born out of due time. (Emphasis mine)

The First Element: Christ died for our sins. The mess we "enjoy" is caused by sin. Whether it's war between nations, friction between us and others or the unseen battle that rages in our souls, it all begins with sin—our rebellion against God and His Word. Christ came to pay a debt of sin we can never pay and offers us eternal life. Our first step toward a new life is a recognition of our sin and the resulting separation from God.

The Second Element: Christ was buried. What's the point? Christ really died. Christ died on Friday afternoon (my understanding). He was buried before six p.m. that day.

The Third Element: Christ rose on the third day. He rose from the dead on a Sunday morning and returned victorious over sin and death.

The Fourth Element: Christ was seen alive! Over 500 people became eyewitnesses of His resurrection.

What are the steps you need to take? First, you must recognize that your sin separates you from a holy God and acknowledge your sin to the Lord. God calls this repentance. Then you must trust Christ alone as your Savior and Sin-bearer.

Not only did the death of Christ provide a great salvation for us for eternity, but He also gives real life to us in our daily lives. In John 10:10, Jesus paints a great portrait of our purposeful life in real time!

The thief does not come except to steal, and to kill, and to destroy. I have come that they may have life and that they may have it more abundantly.

When I placed my faith in Jesus Christ alone as my Savior and Sin-bearer, I finally discovered the "WHY" of life. My "WHY" is to know Christ, to grow in Christ and to help others know Him.

Reading this book can help you build better relationships with people. However, deep peace only flows from this relationship with Christ. If you have not trusted Christ, please do so.

Peace with our Families

Broken families, homes and relationships run rampant around us as our society continues to unravel. Amid the carnage, our Lord Jesus Christ invites us to find rest in Him alone.

Come to Me, all you who labor and are heavy laden, and I will give you rest. Take My yoke upon you and learn from Me, for I am gentle and lowly in heart, and you will find rest for your souls. For My yoke is easy, and My burden is light."

You cannot control or change another person, but Christ Jesus can transform you. Allow Him to shape you. Then, through you, allow Him to transform loved ones and friends as they see the reality of Christ in you!

Flashpoints of Conflict That Impact You

We named a large number of issues that can potentially cause conflict between us and others. Which of those flashpoints affect you the most? Have you let those smoking embers smolder too long? Do not wait until a conflagration breaks out. Where do you need to act? When? Pray about the responsibilities you bear in the friction that separates you from those you know. Pray and ask the Lord for wisdom on how best to broach the subject. Place a date for each issue and resolve to meet with your antagonists by that date. Write them in the space below. Pray before entering these conversations. Then act!

Break the Sound Barrier

Far too many people are timid when it comes to conflict. Many are passive or evasive. Rather than deal with a broken fence, they sulk, become sour, and slowly die inside.

Once again, write down areas where you swallowed your pain and endured grief. Resolve to break the sound barrier. After all, when you refuse to do so, you make yourself a prisoner!

The Objective and Keys to Peacemaking

Remember, the objective of peacemaking is the restoration of broken relationships. Our world is full of them, and you are not immune. The issues could be gossip around the breakroom, people who undermine coworkers to get ahead, classmates who cheated to gain an advantage over you, political or moral divisions in your family or any host of other painful challenges.

Please write down any broken relationships that you wish to restore.

Then, remember the keys to effective peacemaking.

- Keep the circle small. Do not include any "friends" or others to get them on your side. That produces—sides!
- Own your own. If you are the problem, own it.
- Apply the proper passage to your particular problem.
- You know, you go. It's important for those who are aware of issues to deal with those issues. We cannot be like the "see no evil, hear no evil, speak no evil" monkeys. We must act.

Consider the Major Passages and Act on Them as Required

What issues do you face?

- Have you sinned against another? Then go and own it. Matthew 5:21-26

- Has another individual damaged you?
  Matthew 18:15-18

- Civil lawsuits? 1 Corinthians 6:1-11

- Have you caught someone with their hand in the cookie jar? Galatians 6:1 & 10

- A disorderly brother or coworker?
  2 Thessalonians 3:6-15

- Sexual immorality in a church? Galatians 5:1-8

- False teaching and blasphemous (slanderous) speech? 1 Timothy 1:18-20 and 2 Timothy 2:1-18

- Discipline for a sinful leader? 1 Timothy 5:19-20

- Dealing with divisive people? Titus 3:1-11

- Stopping gossip? Proverbs 18:20-21, 26:20-22

- Extend forgiveness as you have been forgiven?
  Ephesians 4:30

Stubborn People Who Refuse to Make Peace

What if people do not respond to you and your overtures to make peace with them? Here is where Romans 12:17-18 comes into play.

> Repay no one evil for evil. Have regard for the good things in the sight of all men. If it is possible, as much as depends on you, **live peaceably with all men**. Beloved, do not avenge yourselves, but rather give place to wrath; for it is written, Vengeance is Mine, I will repay," says the Lord. (emphasis mine)

Do your part. Leave the results to God!

In a Firestorm of Conflict

On occasion, groups find themselves so deeply embroiled in conflict that they can see no way forward. In this case, find a seasoned peacemaker or mediator to help you see, own and conquer the divisiveness.

My Prayer for You

My prayer is that you are making the transition from the pits of unforgiveness and broken relationships to the mountain heights of the forgiven who forgives. Oh, how our world needs people who will Mend Fences. Will you become one of these? Seek the face of God, pray, and take the necessary steps to mend those relationships before time passes and reconciliation is too late. The sand in the hourglass slips away quickly. Act while you still have time. Do not leave fences unmended that need attention. Act now so you won't live with regret when the last grain of sand trickles through the opening.

DR. GORDON E. PENFOLD

Dr. Gordon E. Penfold, B.S, M.S (Colorado State University, 1972, 1973), Th.M. (Dallas Seminary, 1981) and D.Min. (Talbot Theological Seminary, Biola, 2011).

Gordon grew up in a "church" environment. However, he does not remember hearing the gospel until his freshman year as an engineering student at Colorado State University. Two men associated with the Navigators clearly shared the gospel with him. On March 28, 1969, Gordon trusted Jesus Christ as his Savior. He then attended First Baptist Church in Fort Collins, Colorado, where a real, living church captured his heart, mind, and ministry imagination!

Dr. Penfold dreamed of becoming a consulting structural engineer. However, the Lord began to stir his heart to invest his life in people who will live forever instead of investing in buildings and bridges that are temporary (see Revelation 6:12-14 for the description of the *great* coming earthquake). Thus, after a bachelor's and master's degree in engineering and six-and-a-half years working as a structural engineer that included becoming a Registered Professional Engineer, he left engineering behind to become a full-time pastor.

Gordon began full-time ministry in 1980. He pastored four turn-around churches along with four intentional interims. He has trained pastors in the United States, Ukraine, Russia, Armenia, Thailand, Africa, and Singapore. His dissertation, "Defining Characteristics of Turnaround Pastors among Evangelical Churches in the Rocky Mountain States," led to the publishing of

Re:Vision: The Key to Transforming Your Church (Baker Books), co-authored with Dr. Aubrey Malphurs. He and Dr. Gary McIntosh introduced Turnaround Pastor Boot Camps© in 2012, an equipping ministry he continues to develop with Drs. Lavern Brown and Gary Westra. Together these three continue to lead groundbreaking research into effective pastoral ministry practices. They published their innovative research in a new book: *Pastor Unique: Becoming a Turnaround Leader* (WestBow, 2016). His third book: *Restart Churches: A Proven Strategy to Restore Vibrant Ministry in Your Church* (ChurchSmart), was published in June 2020. Gordon serves as the executive director of Fresh Start Ministries that assists plateaued, declining, and conflicted churches discover new life and vibrancy in ministry. He is also the co-founder of Turnaround Pastor, Inc. (now Advanced Pastoral Network). He is the Past President of the Great Commission Research Network, an organization dedicated to understanding effective Great Commission ministry practices and extending those ministry practices worldwide.

By God's grace, he desires to impact the Church of Jesus Christ by further equipping the leaders of churches, the pastors, with tools for effective ministry. Boot camps, online training, and individual coaching and mentoring are the vehicles he desires to use to help revitalize churches. After he attended the Global Proclamation Congress in Bangkok in June 2016, Gordon's vision expanded to include equipping pastoral trainers to impact a growing number of pastors worldwide. This multiplication ministry follows the pattern of 2 Timothy 2:2.

Gordon married his wonderful wife, Beth, in 1970. They have three grown children and four grandchildren. All their children are deeply immersed in ministry as they serve our Lord Jesus Christ. Gordon's life is, indeed, blessed of God!

Fresh Start
M I N I S T R I E S

STRATEGIC CHURCH CONSULTING

Fresh Start Ministries, by design, impacts pastors and churches for greater ministry effectiveness. We provide numerous tools and training that enable pastors and churches to move from plateau and decline to new growth and vitality. Services include:

- Church Consultations and Interventions
- Pastoral Assessments
- Pastoral Coaching and Mentoring
- Advanced Pastoral Training
- Executive Coaching
- Conflict Resolution and Biblical Peacemaking
  - Training for deeply conflicted congregations
  - Conducting Sacred Assemblies that enable churches to resolve sin issues that divide them
  - Seminars for pastors and mid-level judicatories
- Leadership and Church Revitalization Training

FOR MORE INFORMATION
Email: startingfreshnetwork@gmail.com
Phone: (970) 631-6740
Twitter @gordonpenfold
Facebook: Gordon Penfold | Facebook
Website: startingfresh.net

Fresh Start:
Helping to quench the fires of unresolved conflict
Helping to ignite fires of revival in plateaued,
declining and troubled churches

ADVANCED
PASTORAL NETWORK

At Advanced Pastoral Network, we empower church leaders with the critical tools and insights needed to effectively lead their congregations. Our customized coaching programs and cutting-edge strategies cultivate sustainable church growth and enduring leadership.

The Advanced Pastoral Network focuses on five essential facets of ministry to equip pastors and churches for maximum ministry effectiveness.

1. Advanced Pastoral Assessment, Training and Coaching Pastors
2. Church Planter Assessment, Training and Coaching
3. Executive Coaching
4. Church Assessments
5. Pastoral Placement

Contact me at
gordon@turnaroundpastor.com
or check out our website at
https://www.advancedpastoralnetwork.com/

ADDITIONAL RESOURCES

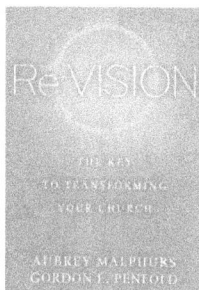

Re:VISION, a comprehensive blueprint for revitalizing stuck churches, focuses on the church's most essential element for transformation—the pastor.

Pastor Unique II directs a pastor to examine their own unique personality and ministry skills to maximize their ministry effectiveness. This book helps pastor unleash their identity and personality to become a revitalization leader in their church.

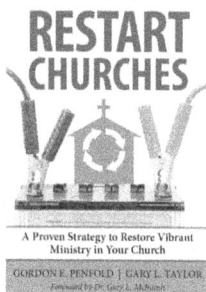

Many churches find themselves running out of resources—people and finances. *RESTART CHURCHES* provides a recipe to help churches successfully navigate the challenges of decline and to develop a vibrant ministry future.

A Prayer For Sam (unpublished)
One family's journey through the anguish of drug addiction

Discovering the Lord—Discovering and Developing a Personal Relationship with the Lord

Discovering the Lord—Leader's Guide